A GENEALOGICAL HISTORY OF THE SCOTT FAMILY

Descendants of Alexander Scott
Who Came to Augusta County, Virginia
circa 1750

with a
History of the Families
with Which They Intermarried

Compiled by
Josephine McCord Vercoe

HERITAGE BOOKS
2011

HERITAGE BOOKS
AN IMPRINT OF HERITAGE BOOKS, INC.

Books, CDs, and more—Worldwide

For our listing of thousands of titles see our website
at
www.HeritageBooks.com

A Facsimile Reprint
Published 2011 by
HERITAGE BOOKS, INC.
Publishing Division
100 Railroad Ave. #104
Westminster, Maryland 21157

International Standard Book Numbers
Paperbound: 978-1-58549-515-3
Clothbound: 978-0-7884-8805-4

Grateful acknowledgments are extended to descendants of the families listed whose assistance and interest have made this record possible.

Miss Helen Wesp, whose address is R. F. D. 16., Box 382, Indianapolis, Indiana, a descendant of James Scott of Richwood, is writing a Scott family history and will greatly appreciate additional records of the families listed from page 1 through page 40.

The compiler, whose address is 2479 Fair Ave., Bexley, Columbus, Ohio, will also appreciate additional records of all families listed.

TABLE OF CONTENTS

TABLE OF CONTENTS

TABLE OF CONTENTS

TABLE OF CONTENTS

FAMILY   PAGE

TABLE OF CONTENTS

TABLE OF CONTENTS

The family of Alexander Scott
and his wife
_____Scott.

Alexander Scott married _____. He died in Augusta
County, Virginia in 1751. Listed as tithable 1750.
Their children were:

1. James, born 1723 or earlier; died 1753;
        unmarried.

2. John, born ca 1725; died 1751; married
        Judith _____.

3. Sarah, born ca 1727; married Jonathan
        Arnold.

4. Phoebe, born ca 1729; married "Irish
        Billy" Cunningham. Lived in
        Hardy Co., Va.

5. Rachael, born ca 1731.

6. Adonijah, born ca 1733; died 1755 in
        Hampshire Co., Va.

7. Benjamin, born ca 1735; died 1790;
        married Mary _____. Lived
        in Hardy Co., Va.

8. David, born 1731; died 1814 near Morgan-
        town, W. Va.; married Judith
        Cunningham.

Appraisors on Inventory (Alexander Scott)

    Daniel Richardson
    Joel Hornbeck
    John Sea
    John Coningham (Cunningham)

The family of John Scott
and his wife
Judith_____.

John Scott, son of Alexander and _____ Scott, was
born ca 1725; died 1751; was first executor of the
estate of Alexander Scott; married Judith _____.
Their children were:

1. James (of Richwood), born 1744; died
        Jan. 1781; married Elizabeth
        _____.

2. Joseph, (may have been Marshall of
        Hampshire county, Va.

3. John, was said to have been killed in
        the Revolutionary War.

4. Jacob, born 1748; died 1808; married
        Catherine Morgan, daughter
        of Zackwell Morgan, founder
        of Morgantown, W. Va.
        He was known as Jacob Scott
        of Red Bridge.

The family of James Scott of Richwood
and his wife
Elizabeth _____.

James Scott, son of John and Judith (Davis) Scott,
was born ca 1744; died January 1781. He received one
thousand acres of land known as the Richwood tract
for his services in the French and Indian Wars, Dec.
1774, under Lord Dunmore. The Richwood tract is between Scotts Meadow Run and Scotts Mill Run. When the
patent was granted the branch had no name. Laurel Point,
Scotts Run (later called Dents Run) and the Richwood
tract were one and the same. This land is about five
miles from Morgantown, in Monongalia County, W. Va.
James Scott headed the Minute Men Oct. 23,1775 according
to information from Public claims of Revolutionary records. His will was made Nov. 1780. Elizabeth, wife of
James Scott was listed in the first census of Monongalia
County as head of the household, comprised of five whites
and two slaves (blacks). December 1, 1803 noted Widow
Scott in the Pindall estate. The children of James Scott
of Richwood and Elizabeth _____ Scott his wife were:

1.   Judith, born 1766, died 1793; married
        Thomas Pindall, son of Capt.
        Phillip Pindall. Thomas Pin-
        dall died May 19, 1795. His
        first wife was Elizabeth
        Harrison who was killed by the
        Indians. She was fifteen years
        of age at her fathers death and
        then received the Crookin Place.
        Both are buried at the head
        waters of Birchfield Run on the
        present Lowe farm near Lowes-
        ville, W. Va.

2.   David, (known as Major David) was born
     in 1786; died March 13, 1846.
     Married first, Rachel _____,
     second, Mary Brand.

3.   Jemima, born 1771; married first Edward
     Pindall, son of Capt. Phillip
     Pindall, married second; ____
     Hess of Mannington, W. Va.

4.   Hannah, born 1779; married William Chipps,
     son of Thomas and Joanna Chipps.

The original land grant for Colonial Service of James

Scott is filed in Richmond, in Augusta Book, page 574.

Land office records.

James Scott was Lieutenant in the 13th Va. Regiment.

Will of James Scott (of Richwood).

In the name of God Amen, I James Scott of Monongalia County, in the State of Virginia, being at the time in a low state of health, but of sound mind, do hereby declare this to be my last will and testament, revoking all former wills that have been made by me, and the first thing I give my soul to the Almighty and my body to the grave to be buried in a decent Christian like manner.

I do hereby appoint my dear brother Jacob Scott and my Uncle David Scott to be executors of my estate, real and personal.

I give and bequeath to my loving wife Elizabeth Scott one rone mare besides what the law allows. I give and bequeath to my best beloved son David Scott the plantation where I formerly lived on the west side of the Monongalia River. I give and bequeath to my daughter Judith Scott, that tract of land known by the name of Crookin Place. I give and bequeath to my daughter Jemima Scott the place I now live on in the Forks, and I give and bequeath to my daughter Hannah Scott an equal share of land not mentioned in the will to be as valuable share as the rest of my children has out of what I own, not mentioned herein.

Witness whereof I have hereunto set my hand and affixed my seal this 25th day of November 1780.

his

James x Scott

Will of James Scott of Richwood Cont'd.

Signed, sealed in the presence of John Burroughs,
James Johnston and John Evans.
Bill states James died January, 1781; all of the
children being infants: Judith age 15; David age
13; Jemima about 10; Hannah about 2. He owned
the Richwood tract. See Chancery file, 1807.

Note:

This will on file at University of W. Va.
library, Morgantown, W. Va.

The family of Judith (Scott) Pindall
and her husband
Thomas Pindall.

Judith Scott Pindall, daughter of James Scott of

Richwood and his wife Elizabeth _____, was born 1766,

died 1793; married Thomas Pindall, son of Capt. Phil-

lip Pindall.   Thomas Pindall died May 19, 1795.

The children of Judith (Scott) Pindall and her husband

Thomas Pindall were:

1.   James, born 1783; died Nov. 22, 1825.
        He was a celebrated lawyer
        and lived in Clarksburg, W. Va.

2.   Elizabeth, born 1787, died 1849; married
        Forbes Britton. Their children
        were:
            Forbes Britton Jr., died 1861.
            Phillip Britton
            Alexander Britton.

3.   Rachel, born 1789; died after 1803;
        married Major Thomas P. Moore.

4.   Jemima, born 1793; died 1866; married
        George I. Davisson.

The family of James Pindall
and his wife
_____ Summerville.

James Pindall had quite a wide reputation as a
lawyer and an orator. He was very eccentric and
many anecotes are told of him which are very amus-
ing. I have seen in the old County court book
records where he was fined for swearing in the
presence of the court. He was a member of the
Virginia legislature at Richmond and in Congress
about 1820. He died in 1826, aged about 45 years.
He married a daughter of John Summerville.

The family of Jemima Pindall
and her husband
George Davisson.

Jemima Pindall, daughter of Judith Scott and

Thomas Pindall was born in 1793. She married

George Davisson.

Their children were:

1.　Rachel.

2.　Edward, married Ann Harrison.

3.　Granville.

Granville Davisson was for many years clerk of

the court of Harrison County, W. Va.

His son George Davisson was a prominent citizen

of Lewis County and represented it in the Legis-

lature.

The family of Rachel Pindall
and her husband
Thomas P. Moore.

Rachel Pindall, daughter of Judith (Scott) and Thomas
Pindall, was born 1793; died 1852; married Major Thomas
P. Moore who was an officer in the War of 1812.
Their children were:

1. Delia Ann Moore who married Luther Haymond
   and lived in Clarksburg, W. Va.

2. Elizabeth Moore who married Lloyd Lowndes
   in 1840.
   Their children were:

   a. Dr. Charles Lowndes.
   b. Richard Tasker Lowndes.
   c. Hon. Lloyd Lowndes, late
      Governor of Maryland.

      (See Lowndes Genealogy,
      Maryland Hist. Mag.,
      Vol. 2 1907).

   d. Clarence Moore Lowndes.

3. Harriett Moore married Waldo P. Goff and
   had three children, one of whom
   was Judge Nathan Goff.

4. Susan Moore married Rev. Leroy B. Gorton,
   a Presbyterian Minister who lived
   in Mississippi.

5. Charles P. Moore married Arabella Tolbert,
   has three children and lives in
   Clarksburg, W. Va.

6. Emily West Moore married Waldo P. Jackson
   of Excello, Missouri.

7. Caroline Moore married James Jackson. They
   have three children who live near
   Clarksburg, W. Va.

8. Thaddeus, unmarried.

Sketch of the Britton family
of
New Jersey___Philadelphia
and
Morgantown, W.Va.

Hannah Salter, daughter of Ebenezer and Rebecca
Stillwell Salter, married Richard Britton of
Monmouth County, N. J. The children of Richard
Britton and his wife Hannah (Salter) Britton were:

1.   Thomas Britton, born 1739.

2.   John Britton, born July 21, 1737.

3.   Rebecca, married Thomas Fleeson
        Jan. 27, 1774.

1.   Thomas Britton, a resident of Philadelphia, was
the son of Richard and Hannah (Salter) Britton; mar-
ried first Catherine Forbes, Sept. 21, 1768, in
Philadelphia, Pa.; married second to Sarah (Salter)
Harvey. The child of Thomas and Catherine (Forbes)
Britton was:

Forbes Britton, who married Elizabeth

Pindall, daughter of Thomas and Judith

(Scott) Pindall.   Elizabeth Pindall

Britton died at Baton Rouge, of yellow

fever, contracted while on a visit to

her son, Capt. Forbes Britton of the

7th Infantry, U.S. Army.

(See sketch of family of Thomas
and Judith Scott on preceding
page).

The line of Hannah Salter, who married Richard
Britton is contained in full in Stillwell's
History of New Jersey, Vol. 4, page 212.

This is a fine Colonial line and well worth
research. Hannah Salter (probably a grand-
mother of Hannah Salter Britton) was the
Ancestress of President Abraham Lincoln.

The family of Jemima Scott
and her husband
Edward Pindall.

Jemima Scott, born 1771, was the daughter of James
Scott of Richwood and his wife Elizabeth _____.
She married Edward Pindall, son of Captain Phillip
Pindall.

Their children were:

    1.   Levi who married Hannah Clark,
              Feb. 19, 1820.

    2.   Elizabeth who married Thomas
              Barnes, Jr., Feb. 12,
              1820.

She married second, _____ Hess of Mannington, W. Va.

Their children were:

    1.   Scott Hess, who married Asenath Hall,
              daughter of John Hall, Aug. 8,
              1831.

    2.   Jemima Hess who married Isaac Boggess.
              Their son Newton Boggess mar-
              married Mary Smith.

The family of Hannah Scott
and her husband
William Chipps.

Hannah Scott, born 1779, daughter of James Scott of
Richwood and Elizabeth _____ Scott his wife, married
William Chipps, son of Thomas and Joanna Chipps.
Their children were:

1. David Chipps.

2. Judith, married Peter Hess.

3. Forbes Britton Chipps married Rachel
    Scott. They were cousins,
    she having been the daughter
    of Major David Scott.

4. Luther Bazell Chipps.

5. Jemima Chipps.

6. Elizabeth Chipps, married first Ed.
    Wilkins; married second
    _____.

7. Franklin S. Chipps, born 1816; died
    1873; married Elizabeth Frum
    Oct. 16, 1838.

8. William Chipps, died ca 1852; married
    _____.
    Their children were:
    Elizabeth, who married
    J. H. Blaney and lives
    in Masontown, W. Va.
    Joanna, who married Henry
    Sapp.

9. Evaline, married Peter Hess?

The family of Franklin S. Chipps
and his wife
Elizabeth Frum

Franklin S. Chipps, son of Hannah Scott and her
husband William Chipps, was born in 1816; died
Sept. 24, 1873; married Elizabeth Frum.
Their children were:

1. Catherine, who married James Austin.

2. William J. died aged 4 years.

3. Lavina Ann, married first James
      Crickett; second, Ellis
      Powell.

4. Rebecca Lee, married Henry Yost.

5. Samantha Ann, married Isaac Austin.

6. Hannah Jane, married Jonathan Powell.

7. John F., married Helen Holland, lives
      in Uffington, W. Va., age 84
      in 1938.

8. Andrew J., died aged 4 years.

9. Horatio Nelson Maxie, died 1933 aged
      72 years; married Theressa
      Howell.

Captain Phillip Pindall.

Phillip Pindall, born in Prince George County, Maryland 1731; died in Monongalia County, West Virginia, 1804; Captain in Col. Lemuel Barrett's Regiment, Maryland Militia; married Rachel Shelby McFarland. Their children were:

1. Jacob, born 1757, died 1829; married Hannah Roberts Chipps.

2. Thomas, married first Elizabeth Harrison, second, Judith Scott, daughter of James Scott of Richwood.

3. Edward, married Jemima Scott, daughter of James Scott of Richwood.

4. Rachel, married John Combs (Coombs) and had two sons:

    a. Phillip.
    b. Joseph.

N. B.

The estate of Captain Phillip Pindall called for settlement December 1, 1803, states he outlived his sons Thomas and Edward and his grandson, Levi. Mentioned in this settlement were: James and Jacob Scott, John Hamilton, Widow Scott (wife of James Scott of Richwood) Morgans, Lemasters, Dawsons, Cochrans and etc.

The family of Phoebe Scott
and her husband
Balser Hess.

Phoebe Hess, daughter of Major David Scott and his first wife, Rachael _____, married Balser Hess. Their children were:

1. Mary Ann, married Dec. 24, 1838 to Stephen Glasscock.

2. Elizabeth, married April 7, 1841 to George Hite.

3. Julia Ann, married Feb. 13, 1841 to Marcus Fetty.

4. Lucinda, married William Chesney (her Uncle by marriage). Their children are listed on a preceding page.

5. David Scott.

6. Rachel Caroline, married Raleigh Dawson; he was the son of Elizabeth Clayton and her husband, George Dawson. Elizabeth Clayton was the daughter of Elijah Clayton and his first wife. Elijah Clayton served in the Revolutionary War from Monmouth, N.J. (see page 488, Hist. of Monongalia Co. by Wiley for proof).

7. Peter, married Evaline Chipps (his cousin).

8. Harriett Jane, married Dr. William N. Dent.

9. Alexander.

The Family of

Jacob Scott of Redbridge

Jacob Scott of Redbridge, son of John and Judith D.
Scott, was born in Hampshire County, Va., in 1748;
died in Monongalia County, Va., in 1808. He served
in the Revolutionary War as a spy and private from
Monongalia County. He married Catherine Morgan,
daughter of Zackwell Morgan and his first wife, Nancy
Paxton. Zackwell Morgan was one of the founders of
Morgantown and a brother of David Morgan. Zackwell
Morgan's first wife, Nancy Paxton, was the mother of
Catherine and two other daughters. All of the other
children were by the second wife, Druscilla Springer.
The children of Jacob and Catherine (Morgan) Scott
were:

1. Phoebe, who married Benjamin Hamilton.
   Their children were:

   a. Jacob Scott Hamilton, who
      married Margaret Pratt,
      daughter of John Pratt,
      Apr., 11, 1820. Their
      children were:
      Sarah,
      John,
      Phoebe,
      Caleb,
      Jane.
   b. William
   c. Ann, who married Caleb Tanzey.
   d. Susannah.
   e. Thomas.
   f. Aaron, who married Jan., 19,1839
      to Nancy Knotts; he died
      in the War with Mexico.
   g. Benjamin, who died in the War
      with Mexico.
   h. Robert.

Captain Phillip Pindall.

The record of Phillip Pindall is unique in that he had served many years in the ranks of the Colonial Troops defending the English against the French and Indians and then became an officer in Washington's army to protect the new republic from the English. Phillip Pindall had thirty-one years of continuous service. He enlisted first in Capt. Alexander Bell's company of Virginia Colonial troops and accompanied General Braddock on his ill-fated expedition to wipe out the French and Indians at Fort Duquesne. He was present at the slaughter at Duquesne and later at the death of General Braddock on the National Highway. Colonel Washington of the Braddock expedition later became General Washington of the American Army. He knew the value of the men of the Virginia Colonial regiment and he desired them for his officers in his newly formed Revolutionary force. In this manner Sergeant Pindall of Capt. Bell's old company became Captain Pindall of the Maryland line.

The question is often asked why Phillip Pindall came from Maryland to the banks of the Monongahela. It is answered by the fact that his land patent presented to him for his service in the war was for a tract which took in practically all of the land between Morgantown and Rivesville on the west bank of the river and extended far into the interior,

Captain Phillip Pindall Cont'd.

at a point about midway of the tract along the river and
a short distance from its banks where a fine spring of-
fered plenty of water, the old fighter settled and raised
his family. There his body is buried amid the graves of
his wife, his children and many other relatives.

Thomas Chipps and his wife Joanna.

Thomas Chipps died ca 1806; his widow Joanna married

second _____ Lucas; she died 1825.

The children of Thomas and Joanna Chipps were:

1.   Hannah Roberts Chipps, who married in 1817
        Jacob Pindall, a Revolutionary soldier.
        (See Pa. Archives, Series 6, Vol. 2,
                         Page 43).

    Their children were:

    a.   Susannah M. Pindall who married
        Josiah Boyers Apr. 25, 1831.

    b.   Hannah Pindall, born 1796; mar-
        ried Daniel Haymond May 30, 1835.

    c.   Elizabeth Pindall, born 1798;
        married Phillip Coombs Oct. 11,1817.

    d.   Rachel Pindall, born 1793, died 1819;
        married Thomas Barnes Oct. 11, 1811.

    e.   Joanna Pindall, born 1792; married
        William Lowman Jan. 15, 1810.

    f.   Thomas Pindall, born 1799; married
        Lurema Swearingen, widow of Samuel
        P. Ray March 19, 1820.

    g.   Evan Shelby Pindall, born 1801; died
        1890; married Druscilla Morgan Barker,
        daughter of Aaron Barker, Dec. 27,1831.

    h.   Ruhama Pindall, born 1808; married
        Gustavus Cresap Feb. 3, 1831.

    Jacob Pindall was born Sept. 1, 1757; died
    Feb. 24, 1829 in Monongalia County, W. Va.
    Hanna Chipps Pindall was born 1771, died
    1851.

2.   John Chipps, who married Hannah _____.

3.   William Chipps, who married Hannah Scott, daughter
        of James Scott of Richwood.

The family of Thomas Chipps and his wife Joanna Cont'd.

4.   Elizabeth Chipps, married Simeon Royce.

5.   Amos Chipps married _____.

6.   Thomas Chipps, married Rachel _____.

7.   Joanna Chipps, married _____ Flowers.

The family of Major David Scott
and his first wife
Rachael _____.

David Scott, born 1768; died March 13, 1846, son of James
Scott of Richwood and his wife Elizabeth _____. He was Major
in the Militia of 1796 with the 4th Regiment of Virginia Reg-
ulars in Ohio County, Va. from 1805 through 1812. He headed
the detachment from his regiment that joined Col. Leftwich at
Point Pleasant, Va. to form the Western Brigade of Virginia.
He left October 2, 1812 for Maumee River near Toledo to join
Maj. Gen. William H. Harrison and to build Fort Meigs. The
children of Major David Scott and his first wife Rachael _____
were:

1. Judith, born Dec. 27, 1799; died June 15, 1863.
   Married David Bouslog.

2. Maria, married Enoch Hoffman.

3. Jacob, born Jan. 1812; married Rachael Neely.
   Died in Lee County, Iowa.

4. Enoch, married Jane Neely. (Rachael and Jane
   were daughters of James Neely).

5. Jemima married Joseph Neely, son of James Neely.

6. Cintha married Eli Fortney.

7. James.

8. Jefferson was in "Mountain Boys of Virginia" 1847.

9. Rachael married her cousin Forbes Britton Chipps.

10. Phoebe married Balser Hess.

11. Catherine married Henry Barrackman.

12. Hannah married William Chesney. She was born
    Sept. 22, 1805; died Sept. 1845.

The family of John Bouslog
and his wife
Catherine _____ Bouslog.

John Bouslog was born ca 1756 in Alsace, Germany; died
in Henry County, Indiana, aged 99 years. He married
Catherine ____, who was born ca 1758 in Germany; died
1855 in Henry County, Indiana, aged 97 years.

John, Rolla (Rawley), and Boston Bouslog, came to
New York in 1780-85. There they separated to look for
a place to settle and agreed to return in six months.
One went north, one west and one south. Rolla never re-
joined them and it is not known what became of him.

In 1814 John Bouslog was one of the trustees of the
newly plotted town of Granville, Va., which was laid out
by Felix Scott, on land he received from his grandfather
Capt. David Scott. John Bouslog owned at least three lots
in the town and a residence.

In 1832 John and Catherine Bouslog and all of their
children came to Henry County, Indiana. There they all
acquired land. Boston Bouslog and his son Rolla came
along with the family of John Bouslog. Nothing more is
recalled of them. Rolla and his brother John practiced
medicine. Both buried in the Harvey cemetery.

John Bouslog's land was near Mt. Summit, Henry Co.

In 1855 John and Catherine Bouslog died and are buried
in Harvey Cemetery, five miles north of Newcastle, Ind.

The family of John and Catherine Bouslog Cont'd.

The Bouslog Bible was printed in Switzerland in 1720.
It is a very large book and in the German language. In it
in beautiful script is a paragraph stating that the Bible
was rebound in Monongalia Co., Va., in 1796.   It was re-
covered with calfskin. Also, that the Bible was to go to
his son David. David died before his father and it was in
the hands of the youngest son, Levi, a miller, for many years.
The sister Dorothy secured it and it is in the hands of her
descendents (1938). It will probably be placed in the Henry
County Historical Museum. Birth dates of all the children of
John and Catherine Bouslog are contained therein.
The children of John and Catherine Bouslog were:

1. Daniel, born July 29, 1794.

2. David, born June 23, 1796, married Judith
            Scott, daughter of Major David Scott.

3. Dorothy, born June 3, 1801; married Adolph
            Lynch. Married second _____ Meeks.

4. Rachael, born Jan. 20, 1805, married Jessee
            Mercer.

5. Catherine, born July 6, 1807, married John
            Boring.

6. Rawley, born Feb. 14, 1810.

7. Levi, born Apr. 25, 1813; went to Oklahoma
            when he was old with some of his
            children.

The family of Judith Scott
and her husband
David Bouslog.

Judith Scott, born December 27, 1799; died June 13, 1863;
married David Bouslog, who was born June 23, 1796; died
in the summer of 1838. He was the son of John and Catherine Bouslog. Judith Bouslog and husband David were
buried in the old graveyard but were moved about 1921 to
the Newcastle Indiana Cemetery by the grandchildren.
The children of Judith and David Bouslog were:

1. John, married Amanda Davis. He was born
   in W. Va., died in Illinois.

2. Strother married twice. Born in W. Va.,
   1824, died in Iowa.

3. Abraham Wesley, born 1826; died 1863; married Amanda _____ _____.

4. Catherine, born 1828 in W. Va., died 1863;
   married Simeon Hays.

5. Rachael, born 1830 in W. Va., died in 1915;
   married Joseph Ellison. Went to
   Nebraska.

6. Mary Jane, born 1832; died 1916; married
   John Vestal, a physician in Newcastle, Ind. They had two sons,
   William and Frank. She married
   second Andrew J. Griffith of
   Deleware. He died in 1907, aged
   76.

7. Enoch, born August 1836 in Indiana; died
   1915 in Newcastle, Inc.; married
   Sarah Coffman. Married second
   Virginia Smith.

The family of Mary Jane Bouslog
and her first husband
John Vestal.

Mary Jane Bouslog, daughter of Judith (Scott) Bouslog

and David Bouslog was born Feb. 17, 1825 in Monongalia

County, W. Va.; died Jan. 1916 in Indianapolis, Ind.

She married Dr. John Vestal (M.D) and they lived in

Newcastle, Ind. Dr. Vestal was born in North Carolina;

died in Newcastle, Ind. in 1863.

Their children were:

1.   Frank Vestal, married Nancy _____,
              their children were:
                   Eugene .
                   Everett.
                   Frank.
                   Chester.

2.   William, married Fanny _____, their
              child was Estelle.

The family of Mary Jane Bouslog
and her second husband
Andrew J. Griffith.

Mary Jane (Bouslog) Vestal, widow of John Vestal,
married second Andrew Jackson Griffith, son of James
and Elizabeth DeHority Griffith. He was born in Kent
County, Delaware, and came to Indiana in 1852; died
Nov. 7, 1907. Mary Jane Bouslog Vestal Griffith and
her second husband, A. J. Griffith are buried in Crown
Hill Cemetery, Indianapolis, Ind.
Their children were:

1. Letta May who married Stephen Miller.

2. Harriett G. (twin) born June 29, 1869;
married Henry Harmon Wesp, son
of John and Mary Harmon Wesp.

3. Harry, born June 29, 1869; died 1932.
Married Arminta Hale, daughter
of James and _____ Hale.

4. Jessie Altonia, born June 20, 1871;
married William B. Thompson,
son of Burdine and Sarah Tignor
Thompson; died 1923.

The family of Harriett Griffith Wesp
and her husband
Henry Harmon Wesp

Harriett Griffith, daughter of Andrew J. and Mary Jane
(Bouslog) Griffith, was a twin. She married Henry Harmon
Wesp, son of Mary Ann Harmon and John West. She was born
June 29, 1869 in Anderson, Ind. Mary Ann Harmon was the
daughter of Adam and Wilhlemina (Frey) Harmon; and John
Wesp was the son of John and _____ Wesp.
Harriett Griffith and Henry Harmon West were married
October 27, 1888, in Indianapolis, Ind. Their children
were:

1.   Helen Arminta, not married, born Sept. 3, 1889.

2.   Margaret Jane (twin), born Nov. 22, 1891; mar-
          ried Robert Russel Fohl, son of Bernie
          and _____ Fohl. Their children are:
             Ruth K.
             Robert Russel Jr.
             Margaret Jane.

3.   Ruth Griffith, born Nov. 22, 1891 (twin) married
          Leroy Downs. Lives in Noblesville, Ind.

4.   Catherine Elizabeth, born June 26, 1895; married
          Dec. 24, 1917, to Elias Herbert Thomas,
          son of John Aldis and Jennie Lee Thomas.
          E. H. Thomas was born at Carmel, Ind.,
          died Dec. 1, 1928. Lived on the home
          place in Hamilton Co., Ind. Was a World
          War Veteran. Their children were:

          a.   Herbert Wesp, Feb. 24, 1919.
          b.   John Henry, Dec. 25, 1921
          c.   William Lee, Dec. 9, 1923.
          d.   Griffith Paul, Sept. 10, 1925.
          e.   David Richard, Sept. 3, 1927.
                Named by his Aunt Helen Wesp for
                Major David Scott and David Bouslog.

The family of Harriett Griffith Wesp and her husband,

Henry Harmon West, Cont'd.

    5.   John Andrew Wesp, born November 19,
               1900, married Lela Lentz
               June 29, 1921. Divorced
               1936. Served in the World
               War. No children.

The family of Jesse Altonia Griffith
and her husband
William B. Thompson.

Jessie Altonia Griffith, born June 20, 1871 in Anderson,
Ind.; married William B. Thompson, son of Burdine and
Sarah Ann (Tignor) Burdine Nov. 27, 1898, at Indianapolis,
Ind.

Their children were:

1. Griffith, born October 29, 1901; married
        Dorothy Zimmerman, July 1926 in
        New York. They have a child,
        Amy Zimmerman Thompson, born
        Nov. 1, 1929 in New York.

2. Lindabelle married Burke H. Robinson, son
        of Edward J. and Helen (Pettibone)
        Robinson, May 17, 1932. She was
        born July 28, 1904.

3. Harry J., born Feb. 22, 1910; married Doris
        Pender Dec. 26, 1936 in New York.
        They had twins:
            Linda Thompson, born May 1, 1938.
            Susan Thompson, born May 1, 1938.

The family of Jacob Scott
and his wife
Rachael Neely (Neeley)

Jacob Scott, son of Major David Scott and his first
wife, Rachael _____, was born Jan. 1812. He married
Rachael Neely. He inherited, with Enoch Lemaster, a
tract deeded to them by David and Rachael Scott. He
went to Indiana in 1832; to Iowa in 1843; to Missouri
in 1857. Rachael Scott died there. Jacob Scott returned to Iowa and died there in Lee County.
The children of Jacob and Rachael (Neely) Scott were:

1. Minerva, married _____ Stillwell.

2. Julia Ann.

3. Enoch.

4. David.

5. Rachael married _____ Myers, lived in
    Kansas.

6. Alpheus N., died ca 1883 (Feb.); mar-
    ried his cousin, Mary Huffman.
    Their children were:

    a. Louisa Scott; married
        _____ Myers.
    b. Sarah Scott, married Page
        Stevens.
    c. Jacob Scott.
    d. Amanda Scott, married
        Frank _____.
    e. Harry Scott.
    f. Leroy Scott.

The family of William Chesney and his second wife,
Lucinda Hess Cont"d.

g.   Odell Scott.

Benjamin Chesney, father of William Chesney, was a
Revolutionary Soldier in the south and came from
Rockingham County, Va.; settled on Gustins Run, a
branch of Scotts Run. (Ref. Wiley's History of
Monongalia County, W. Va., page 702, footnote).
Benjamin Chesney was a Dragoon, Lee's Division,
pensioned Oct. 22, 1828.
Lived with William Cole in Monongalia County. Aged
80 years in 1840.

The family of Jemima Scott
and her husband
Joseph Neely.

Jemima Scott, daughter of Major David Scott and his first wife Rachael _____, married Joseph Neeley, son of James Neeley. Their children were:

1. Samuel Neeley

2. Mary Neeley

3. Elizabeth Neeley; married David Reger.

4. Jemima Neeley; married John Cobun.

5. David Neeley

6. Ann Neeley; married _____ Reger and
   lived in Kansas.

7. Sarah Neeley; married William Fleming.

The family of Enoch Scott
and his wife
Jane Neeley.

Enoch Scott, son of Major David Scott and his first

wife Rachael _____, inherited part of the LeMaster

tract which was deeded to him Sept. 12, 1812, by

David and Rachael Scott, his mother and father.   Enoch

lived in Lee County, Iowa.

In a letter written by David Scott Oct. 27, 1844, we

find the following:

        "Enoch is to start in two weeks to go where

Jake is, as Mississippi is a good place to settle".

Enoch Scott married Jan. 7, 1813 Jane Neeley, daughter

of James Neeley of Monongalia County, Va.

Jefferson Scott

Jefferson Scott, son of Major David Scott and
his first wife Rachael _____, never married, it
is believed. He deeded one-half of the land he
inherited (Richwood) in June 1852 to his brother,
Enoch.

In 1853, after the death of his step-mother, he
deeded the other half to James Snyder who had
bought out Enoch's share at the same time. About
1913 John Chisler bought it and is the present
owner of the Major David Scott homeplace.

The family of Rachael Scott
and her husband
Forbes Britton Chipps

Rachael Scott, daughter of Major David Scott and his
wife Rachael _____, married her cousin, Forbes Britton
Chipps, who was the son of Hannah Scott and her husband
William Chipps.

No mention made of children.

The family of Catherine (Caty) Scott
and her husband
Henry Barrickman.

Catherine (Caty) Scott, daughter of Major David Scott
and his wife Rachael _____, was born 1805; married
Henry Barrickman, born 1802, son of John Barrickman
of Cassville, Monongalia County, W. Va.
Caty is mentioned in Major David Scott's letter of
Oct. 27, 1844.
The children of Catherine Scott and Henry Barrickman
were:

1. Miranda, born 1830.

2. Rachael, born 1834.

3. David, born 1835.

4. John, born 1837.

5. Mariah, born 1840.

6. Hannah, born 1842.

7. Mary (twin), born 1847.

8. Strother (twin), born 1847.

9. Francis Ann, born 1849.

The family of Hannah Scott
and her husband
William Chesney.

Hannah Scott, born Sept. 22, 1805; died Sept. 1845;
was the daughter of Major David Scott and his first
wife, Rachael _____.   Hannah Scott married William
Chesney, son of Benjamin Chesney. Their children were:

1. Benjamin; married Lucinda Ann Barb. Their
       children were:

   a. Moses.
   b. David.

2. David, married Lydia _____.

3. Rachael, married _____ Brown.

4. Judith, married _____ Anderson.

5. William Jr.

6. Margaret, married _____ Anderson.

William Chesney married second; Lucinda Hess, daughter
of Phoebe (Scott) Hess and Balser Hess. Their children
were:

1. Phoebe Ann, married Jefferson Tenant.
       Their children are:

   a. Ida May, married S. A. Barker
       (see Jacob of Red Bridge of
       Capt. David Scott's line).
       They live in Morgantown. (1938)
   b. Harriett, unmarried (1938).
   c. Marietta, married _____ Moley?
   d. William Richard.
   e. Abraham W.
   f. Iras Columbia, married _____ Gist.

2.   James, born Sept., 23, 1777; died 1840; married
        Rebecca (Sara) Barker, July 3, 1800.
        Their children were:

        a. James Jr., married Sara Dean.
        b. Joseph, married Arah Goodnight,
            daughter of Christopher (Christian)
            Goodnight.
        c. Felix.
        d. Benjamin, who had a son William,
            who was a minister, residing in
            Fairmont, W. Va.
        e. Jacob, who married Rachael Goodnight.
        f. Catherine.
        g. Phoebe, who married John Neeley.
        h. Elizabeth, who married Oct., 31,
            1836 to John Van Horn.
        i. Sarah.
        j. Nancy, who married _____Davis.

3.   Joseph, who married Phoebe Ridgeway, daughter
        of Noah Ridgeway. Their children were:

                Caroline,
                Jane,
                Sarah,
                Susannah,
                Nancy,
                Thomas.

4.   Morgan, who married Catherine Barker, daughter
        of Joseph Barker. He was in the 3rd Va.,
        Regulars. A daughter Druscilla, married
        June 27, 1836 to David E. West.

5.   Sarah, who married Aaron Barker, son of Joseph
        Barker. Their children were:

        a. Benjamin, who married Rebecca Morgan,
            who was his second cousin.
            She was a daughter of Zackwell
            Morgan, a grandaughter of David
            Morgan. Her father, Zackwell
            Morgan was a nephew of Zackwell
            Morgan, founder of Morgantown.
            Their children were:

                Catherine Barker, who mar-
                ried Ira Hall.

The family of Jacob Scott of Redbridge, Cont'd.

                        Shelby Pindall Barker
                        Sarah Barker
                        Druscilla Barker, who
                        married ____Repplinger.
                        Lina M. Barker, who mar-
                        ried _____McElroy.

b. Druscilla, who married General Evan
            Shelby Pindall, Dec., 27,
            1832.

c. Jacob
d. Joseph
e. Alfred.

The family of Jacob Scott of Redbridge Cont'd.

Joseph Scott, son of Jacob and Catherine (Morgan) Scott married Phoebe Ridgeway (who died in 1851). They married May 18, 1824. Their children, (named on a preceding page) were:

1. Caroline, who married Solomon Newbraugh.
   Their children were:

   a. Mary Jane, who married Henry Youst. They were living near Morgantown in 1938.

   b. John Newbraugh.

2. Sarah Ann, who married Andrew A. Atewart, son of William and Belinda (Jones) Stewart. Their daughter Caroline (Carrie) married Augustus T. Metcalf.

3. Mary Jane Scott married John Steele.

4. Nimrod Scott.

5. Nancy Scott.

6. Tazewell M. Scott.

7. Thaddeus Scott.

Copy of the Act passed by the General Assembly Of

Virginia in October 1785, granting to Zackwell Morgan

the right to lay out and establish a town by the name

of Morgans-town.

(Hening's Statutes at Large, Vol. 12, p. 212.)

1.   Be it enacted by the General Assembly, that

fifty acres of land, the property of Zackwell Morgan

lying in the county of Monongalia, shall be and they

are hereby vested in Samuel Hanway, John Evans, Davis

Scot, Michael Kearns, and James Daugherty, gentlemen,

trustees, to be by them or any three of them, laid out

into lots of half an acre each, with convenient streets

which shall be, and the same are hereby established a

town, by the name of Morgans-town.

The Morgan family.

Col. Morgan Morgan (1688-1766) came from Glamorgan-
shire, Wales, about 1713 and settled at Christina, Delaware;
later near Winchester, Virginia; married in 1714, Catherine
Garretson (1692 - 1733).

Their sons Zackwell and David Morgan settled in Monongalia
County, W. Va., on the site of Morgantown (which they founded)
in 1768.

Col. Zackwell Morgan was born ca 1735 in Frederick, Va.,
died Jan. 1, 1795 in Monongalia Co., (Marion Co.), W. Va. He
lived for a time in Berkeley Co., W. Va.; settled for a time
on George's Creek in Pennsylvania, then went to Morgantown.
Col. Morgan served with Va. forces in the French and Indian
War. Served in the Revolution as Va. County Lieutenant and
Colonel.

Zackwell Morgan married first Nancy Paxton. Their children
were:

    1.   Catherine, who married Jacob Scott.

    2.   Nancy, who married John Pierpont.

    3.   Temperance, who married _____ Cochran.

Zackwell, married second Druscilla Springer, who was the
daughter of Count Carl Christopher Springer, a Swedish nobleman,
who was the founder of Christina, Del. She was said to have
been a sister of Col. Zadoc Springer of Pennsylvania. Their
children, Zackwell Morgan and his second wife Druscilla

The Morgan family, Cont'd.

(Springer) Morgan were:

1.   Levi, the noted scout who died in Ky.

2.   Uriah, who was in Indian warfare, died in
          Tyler Co., W. Va.

3.   James, an Indian fighter.

4.   Zadoc, who died young.

5.   Morgan, who died in Tyler Co., W. Va.

6.   Capt. Zackwell, died at Bladensburg (War 1812)

7.   Hannah, married David Barker.

8.   Sally, married James Clelland.

9.   Rachael.

10. Druscilla, married Jacob Swisher.

The family of Sarah Scott
and her husband
Jonathan Arnold.

Sarah Scott, daughter of Alexander and _____ Scott,
was born ca 1727; married ca 1747 to Jonathan Arnold
of Augusta County, Virginia. They were living there
in 1764. About 1786 they moved to Fayette County, Pa.;
bought land known as "West Bend of Monongahela River"
in Luzerne Township. This land adjoined that of their
son, Jonathan. Their children were:

1.   Jonathan.

2.   Benjamin, married Mary _____.   Had a son
            Rezin, came to Cadiz, Ohio.

3.   Jemima, married Rezin Virgin.

4.   Rachael, married _____ Hammond.

5.   Hannah.

6.   Sarah.

7.   Levi, married Hannah; was a Rev.   Sold.
            (See Official Roster Sold. of
            Rev. who lived in Ohio, Vol. 2.)

8.   William, married Hulda Knotts; lived in
            Greene Co., Pa.

9.   James.

William and James were twins.

The family burial ground is in "West Bend Episcopal
Church Cemetery".

Wills and deeds filed in Uniontown, Pa.

The family of Benjamin Scott
of Hampshire, Randolph
and
Hardy County, Va.

Benjamin Scott, son of Alexander Scott and his wife

_____ Scott, was born ca 1735; died ca 1790 in Hardy

County, Va. He was in Hampshire County in 1754, he, at

the time of his death, had several tracts of land, one

in Randolph Co., Va. He lived opposite Fort Currence,

this plantation was near the Hamilton place. He pur-

chased part of his land from his brother David Scott,

(Capt. David). His will probated in Hardy County lists

his children as follows:

1. Benjamin.

2. John, whose plantation was on the east side of
   Looney's Creek.

3. Alexander, whose plantation was on the west side
   of Looney's Creek; enlisted in Rev. War,
   1780 as spy, was present at the siege of
   Yorktown. In 1832 applied for pension.
   (see Rev. Sold. buried in Ind.). He was
   born 1762 in Hardy Co., Va. Died in Cass
   Co., Ind. 1844.
   His wife was Sarah _____.
   Their children were:
   a. Rev. Alexander Scott (War 1812)
   b. David Scott, born 1784, died 1837.
   c. Sarah A. Dunbar, born 1795, died 1875.
   d. Rev. John Scott, born 1797, died 1866.
   e. Cynthia Wilson, born 1807, died 1861.
   f. Margaret Boyd, born 1809, died 1850.
   g. Polly McLucas _____.

4. Samuel, who lived in Kentucky. His wife was Elizabeth
   Cunningham, daughter of John and Elizabeth
   Cunningham of Hardy Co., Va. John Cunningham
   was a brother of "Irish Billy" Cunningham who
   married Phoebe Scott.

5. Elizabeth.

The family of Benjamin Scott, Cont'd.

      6.   Nancy.

      7.   Hannah.

      8.   Mary.

Witnesses on will:
          R. Cunningham
          Alexander Simpson
          Joseph Welton.

Executors: Benjamin and John Scott.

Note:

Cunningham and Welton names appear on other Scott wills and deeds.

Also in Hardy County, Va. is a will of Rachael Scott, who mentioned daughters Phoebe and Jean. Witnessed by John Scott, Samuel B. Davis and Henry Harrison.

The family of Benjamin Scott, Jr.,
and his wife
Nancy _____.

Benjamin Scott, son of Benjamin and Mary (_____)

Scott of Hardy Co., W. Va., was born May 29, 1754 in

Augusta Co., Va., died in Jackson Co., Ind., Oct. 1840;

married Nancy _____.

Their children were:

1. John.

2. James, born 1781; died before 1820; married
       in 1808 in Kentucky to Susannah Zike.
       Susannah married second, her husband's
       brother, John Scott. The children of
       James and Susannah Scott were:

       a. Samuel.
       b. John P., married Cynthia Dodds.
       c. William, married Mary Wood, they
          had eight children, three of whom
          were: Alexander and Martha, twins,
          a daughter Parthena, who married
          Benjamin Hamilton and removed to
          Calif.
       d. Melinda.
       e. Margaret Catherine, who married
          James W. Croucher.
       f. name unknown.

   Benjamin Scott, Jr., enlisted in Augusta Co., Va.
   March 1777 served as Sergeant for 6 months in
   Capt. Moses Huttons Company of Virginia Troops.
   Discharged at Wheeling, Aug. 1777.
   Enlisted May 1, and served as an Orderly Sgt.
   for two months in Capt. Michael Stumps Co.
   Discharged July 1, 1781.
   Pension Claim, 170761.
   Died 1840 buried on Scott farm, Owen Twp., Jackson
   Co., Ind.

Benjamin and Alexander Scott were brothers, both lived in
Kentucky before locating in Ind. A descendant lives on the
Benjamin Scott place and has supplied these records. He has
the Benjamin Scott Bible.

The Cunningham Family
of the
South Branch

John Cunningham came from Ireland to the South Branch
of the Potomac about 1749 and settled near Moorefield,
Va. With him were three sons and a daughter Judith.
He died about 1757.

His son John married Elizabeth _____, and raised
a large family near Moorefield, at a village called
Cunningham, named for the family.

His son William, called "Irish Billy" married Phoebe
Scott, daughter of Alexander Scott, they also raised their
family there.

His daughter Judith married David Scott, a son of
Alexander Scott. They settled near Morgantown, Monongalia County, W. Va.

His son Robert was said to have lived in Kentucky.

Romney, W. Va.

Deed Book 1, Page 6.

Fairfax grant, given and confirmed to John Cunningham
of the county of Frederick, a tract of land upon the
Wappacoma or the Great South Branch of the Potomac River,
known and distinguished by the number 38 in the plat
survey. Proprietors deed to John Cunningham in 1749.
Registered in the proprietors office in book g at a
court held for Hampshire County, Dec. 13, 1757. This
deed from the Proprietor of the northern neck to John
Cunningham was (on the motion of William Cunningham,
heir at law of John Cunningham) ordered to be recorded.

Test. Gabriel Jones.

Deed Book 1, page 148.

Between William Cunningham and Phoebe his wife and
Thomas Singleton.

Wit. Garrett Van Meter

Benjamin Kukendall

John McCulloch

Dated Nov. 6, 1762.

Note:

This is William Cunningham and Phoebe Scott.

The family of Phoebe Scott
and her husband
William Cunningham.

Phoebe Scott, daughter of Alexander Scott and his
wife _____, married William Cunningham (Known as
"Irish Billy") who was a son of John Cunningham, who
came from Ireland to the South Branch ca 1750.
Some of the children of William and Phoebe (Scott)
Cunningham were:

1. William Jr., who married Jemima Harness.

2. Hannah, who died unmarried.

3. James.

4. Ann.

Sketch of

Adonijah Scott.

Adonijah Scott, was the son of Alexander and _____

Scott. Records of his family (or descendants) are

to be found in Wetzel County, W. Va. in Book 1, page

446. Names listed:

> Samuel Crawford
> James B. Gordon and Elizabeth.
> John M. Scott.
> Evans Rea and Mary, his wife.
> Jacob Rem ? and Susan, his wife.
> Thomas Hill and Jane, his wife.
> David Hill.
> James Hill.

All of North Liberties, Phila. Pa. in 1850.

Dated Sept. 13, 1825.

In Hampshire County, Va., Aug. 17, 1775 a James Scott

and his wife Elizabeth, Davis Scott and his wife Judith,

signed a lease for lands to Felix Seymore. This land

was apparently James Scott's, as heir-at-law of Adonijah

Scott, deceased. This land was patented to Adonijah

Scott, Nov. 13, 1754, by Fairfax on Looney's Creek.

No further records on this family.

The family of Captain David Scott
and his wife
Judith Cunningham.

Captain David Scott, son of Alexander Scott, was born in 1737. He came from the South Branch of the Potomac, Virginia, (now West Virginia), where he died in 1814.

He was the youngest of eight children, was a Baptist and one of the first members of the Forks of Cheat Baptist Church in Monongalia County, W. Va. He served in the Colonial Wars (see land grant, preceding page for his service). He served three years in the Revolution, was Captain of the 13th, Va. Regiment. He received 4000 A. of land and a pension, (see report of Va. State Library, Sup. 1912, page 270. Revolutionary Soldiers of Virginia, 1911, page 392, Pension Department, Washington, D. C.) David Scott was on list of taxable property in 1783 Monongalia County, W. Va.

David Scott and his son James were Justices of the County in 1798. (see Wiley's History of Monongalia County, page 313.)

Captain David Scott married first ca 1760, Judith Cunningham (born ca 1740). The children of Captain David and Judith (Cunningham) Scott were:

1. Phoebe) killed by the Indians in 1779 across
) the river from their home, as they
) carried lunch to the hay harvesters
2. Fanny) in the meadow.

The family of Captain David Scott and his wife, Judith
Cunningham, Cont'd.

3.   Hannah, born 1763, married Jesse Martin, son of
         Col. Charles Martin, builder of Ft.
         Martin, near Morgantown, W. Va.

4.   James, born 1765, married Amelia Daugherty,
         daughter of Capt. James Daugherty.
         He was a soldier of the Revolution
         and the War 1812.

5.   Robert C., married Lydia Rees of the State of
         Delaware.

6.   Sarah (Sally), married Stephen Gapen. She was
         born 1774, died Nov. 12, 1792.

7.   Felix, born 1786; died 1858; married first
         Nancy Ann Dent, daughter of Capt.
         John Dent; married second, Ellen
         Castlio, (Castilo).

8.   Betsy, married Dr. Daniel Merchamd of Uniontown,
         Pa.

9.   Nancy, married George Metcalf.

Captain David Scott married second Clary Byrne, a widow,
about 1797. There were no children by this marriage.

DAVID SCOTT   )   George the third &c., To all &c., Whereas
  1000 A.   )
Monongalia Co.   )   by our Royal Proclamation dated at St.
12-7-1774.   )
From: Patent Bk.   )   James' the Seventh day of October one
No. 42, p. 785   )
                        thousand seven hundred and Sixty-three

in the third year of our Reign for regulating the Cessions made

to us in America by the Late Treaty of peace, we did Command and

Impower our Governors of our several Provinces in North America

to grant without fee or reward to such reduced Officers as had

served in North America during the late war and to such private

Soldiers as had been or should be disbanded in America and are

actually residing there and should personally apply for same,

certain quantities of Land subject at the expiration of Ten

years to the same Quit rents as other Lands are subject to, and

it being sufficiently proved to our Lieutenant and Governor of

our Colony and Dominion of Virginia that Peter Hogg, late a

Captain in the service of the Colony is entitled to three thou-

sand acres of Land under our Royal Proclamation aforesaid, one

thousand Acres part thereof is assigned unto David Scott, KNOW

YE therefore that for the consideration aforesaid WE have Given

Granted and Confirmed and by these presents for us our heirs

and Successors DO Give Grant and Confirm unto the said David

Scott one certain Tract or parcel of Land containing one thou-

sand Acres lying and being in the County of Augusta on the

west side of the Monongalia River and on a branch thereof called

Middle Island Creek and bounded as followeth to-wit, Beginning

at an ash and sugar bushes on the River bank, corner to David

Scott's Land and running with the lines of the same South seven

degrees West one hundred and ten poles to a white oak and
hickory South forty-eight degrees West one hundred and fifty
poles to a white oak and a black oak, corner to Jacob Scott's
Land and with the lines thereof South fifty-nine degrees West
Sixty poles to two white oaks by a Run South Thirty-two degrees West Seventy-eight poles to a Spanish oak and hickory North
Eighty-eight degrees West one hundred and twenty-six poles to a
sugar tree North Seventy degrees West Eighty poles to a white
oak and walnut North Eighty-eight degrees West Seventy poles,
passing a corner of the above land, to a white oak on a hill
side South Twenty-nine degrees West one hundred and Ten poles
to two Spanish oaks South Thirty-four degrees West one Hundred
and Two poles to an Elm and Spanish oak on a Creek and down
the same One Hundred and Thirty-eight poles to a sugar tree
South Sixty-five degrees East Eighty-four poles to two white
oaks by a gully North Thirty-eight degrees East Sixty poles
to an Elm on the Creek North Twenty-eight degrees East One
hundred and Six poles to a white oak North six degrees East
Thirty-two poles to a sugar tree and white Oak North Fifty
degrees East Thirty-two poles to a hickory and Elm on the
Creek South Eighty-three degrees East Sixty-two poles to two
black Oaks South Twenty-three degrees East Fifty-eight poles
to a white Oak and black Oak South Twelve degrees West Twenty
poles to three white Oaks and a Spanish Oak and dogwood on
the end of a hill North Seventy-two degrees East Three
Hundred and Forty-four poles to two white Oaks and a sugar
tree on the River and down the several courses of the same

Four Hundred and Seventy poles to Beginning. WITH ALL &c.
To have, Hold, &c., to be held &c. YIELDING AND PAYING, &c.
IN WITNESS &c. WITNESS our trusty and well beloved John,
Earl of Dunmore our Lieutenant and Governor General of our
said Colony and Dominion at Williamsburg under the Seal of
our said Colony the Seventh day of December One Thousand
seven Hundred and Seventy-four in the fifteenth Year of
our Reign.

                    Dunmore,

Patent Book No. 42, page 785, State Land Office, Capitol
Bldg., Richmond, Va.

The family of Sarah Scott
and her husband
Stephen Gapen.

Sarah Scott, daughter of Captain David and Judith
(Cunningham) Scott, was born March 5, 1774, died
Nov. 12, 1792; married Stephen Gapen, son of Zac-
hariah (born Aug. 10, 1733) and Ruth (Tindall, born
1740) Gapen (who were married July 7, 1760). Nov-
ember 12, 1792, in Mongalia County, Virginia.
The children of Stephen and his first wife Sarah
(Scott) Gapen were:

1.   Francis Gapen, born July 5, 1793; died
         May 5, 1794.

2.   Zachariah Gapen, born July 12, 1795.

3.   Stephen Gapen II, born July 21, 1797.

4.   Judith Gapen (Dent), born Aug. 1, 1799.

5.   Matilda Gapen, born Oct. 21, 1801, died
         Oct. 26, 1804.

6.   Nancy.

Stephen Gapen.

Stephen Gapen, son of Zachariah (b. Aug. 10, 1733)
and Ruth (Tindall, b. 1740) Gapen, (who were married
July 7, 1760), was born May 29, 1761; died Dec. 26,
1838; served in the Revolution as follows:

    1777   enlisted in Captain John Minor's Pennsylvania
            Company and served six months as a private at
            Fort. Pitt under General Hand.

    1778-79 enlisted and served six months as an Indian
             Spy.

    1779   volunteered and served one month under Capt.
            Phillips and Col. Brodhead, Pa. Troops.

    1781   enlisted and served six months and two days
            as Indian Spy under Lieut. James Marshall.

    1782   enlisted and served three months as Indian Spy.

    From 1777 until 1782 his home was on the frontier in
            Washington County, Pa., and in addition to the
            above named tours he rendered about two years
            service in scouting parties whenever called
            upon.

    Was allowed pension on his application, executed Aug.
            27, 1832, while residing in Monongalia Co., Va.

        Ref: Revolutionary War Pension Claim S. 8545.

Stephen Gapen married first Sarah Scott, daughter of Captain
David and Judith (Cunningham) Scott (see preceding page);
married second Rebecca Snider (b. April 17, 1788; died Feb.
19, 1849; See Snider), Jan. 13, 1783 in Monongalia County,
Virginia. The children of Stephen and Rebecca (Snider)
Gapen, were:

    1.   Sarah Gapen, born Jan. 19, 1807.

Stephen Gapen, Cont'd.

2. John Gapen, born March 16, 1809.

3. Josiah Gapen, born July 12, 1810.

4. Dorcas Gapen, March 2, 1812.

5. Amos Gapen, born Oct. 3, 1813.

6. Daniel Gapen, born March 17, 1815; died
    Feb. 15, 1882.

7. Ruth Gapen, born Sept. 25, 1816.

8. Matilda Gapen, born Jan. 3, 1819.

9. Rachael Gapen, born June 24, 1820.

10. Eunice Gapen, born Feb. 6, 1822.

11. Elizabeth Gapen, born Feb. 2, 1824.

12. Thomas Gapen, born Oct. 12, 1826; died
    July 15, 1827.

(Records contributed by Mr. Thomas Ray Dille
 of Morgantown, W. Va.)

The family of John Snider
and his wife
Dorcas (Darcus) Evans.

John Snider, it is said was induced to come out from
Richmond, Va., by a Minor, into Greene County, Pa. to
hunt for him. While out hunting he was captured by
the Indians and taken back to Cass District, and kept
eight years before he was exchanged. He came back
and piloted a company to Crooked Run, showing where
the Indians camped with him over night, some four hundred yards from where Thomas Maple now lives.

John Snider married an Evans (tradition says Darcus
was her name). He took up a tract of land now owned by
Thomas Maple and John Garlow.
Their children were:

1.   Joseph, who located at Farmington.

2.   David, who settled on Big Indian Creek.

3.   Joshua.

4.   Amos.

5.   Thomas, who went to Trumbull Co., Ohio.

6.   Rebecca, who was the second wife of Stephen
     Gapen.

7.   Elizabeth, who married a Billingsly.

8.   Elisha, who married Edith Britton, a daughter
     of Wilson Britton.

See Wiley's Hist. Monongalia Co., W. Va., page 697.

The family of Robert Scott
and his wife
Lydia Rees.

Robert Scott, son of Captain David and Judith

(Cunningham) Scott, married Lydia Rees of Smyrna,

Delaware.

Their child was:

1.   Elizabeth, who married _____ Wildes.
                There were no children.

Charles Martin.

Charles Martin, known to his descendants as Col. Charles
Martin, was a Minuteman and was in command of a Fort on
Crooked Run, in Monongalia County, Virginia (now West
Virginia), not far from Morgantown from 1733 to 1783.
This Fort was built as a defense for the people of Monongalia County against the Indians, but after the Declaration of Independence was signed it was used as a
defense against both British and Indians. It was at-
tacked June 1829 and ten whites were captured and killed.
Charles Martin was granted ten acres of land in Monongalia County in 1769. Although Charles Martin was known as
Col. Charles Martin there seems to be no record justifying
this title.

The family of Col. Charles Martin
and his wife
Elizabeth Burrows.

Col. Charles Martin is said to have come from Eastern Virginia and was first in Union District at Collins Ferry. He is said to have been over six feet high, of dark complexion, with a keen, piercing, black eye. He was born ca 1715; died ca 1790. He resided at Martins Fort on Crooked Run in Monongalia County, W. Va. He married Elizabeth Burrows. Their children were:

1. Jesse, born Crooked Run, Monongalia County, W. Va. and lived there; married Hannah Scott.

2. William, married Hannah Randall, resided near Farmington, W. Va.

3. George, born April 6, 1765; died Dec. 19, 1827; married Elizabeth Hoard; lived near Farmington, W. Va.

4. Presley, resided at New Martinsville, W. Va.; He is said to have been the founder of New Martinsville.

5. Spencer, born March 6, 1772; died Feb. 13, 1849; married first Polly (Mary) Snyder. He married second, Margaret Sturm.

6. Ann, married Richard Harrison.

7. Elizabeth, married Norman Randall.

For family of Jesse Martin and his wife Hannah Scott, see preceding page.

The family of Hannah Scott
and her husband
Jesse Martin.

Hannah Scott, daughter of Captain David and Judith
(Cunningham) Scott, married Jesse Martin, son of
Col. Charles and Elizabeth (Burrows) Martin.
Their children were:

1. Charles, who married Susannah Harrison.

2. Phoebe, who married Caleb Tripett July
   24, 1806.

3. Scott, who married _____ Hoge.

4. Tazwell, who married _____ Bailey.

5. Nancy, who married Moses Rhodes of
   Hardy County, W. Va.

6. Francis, who married _____ Watkins.

7. Sarah, who married _____ Hildebrand.

Charles Martin who married Susannah Harrison had a
daughter Nancy, who married James N. Scott in 1839.
They had a son named Moses Rhodes Scott.

The family of William Martin
and his wife
Hannah Randall.

William Martin, second son of Col. Charles and

Elizabeth (Burrows) Martin, married Hannah Randall.

Their children were:

    1. Tapley.

    2. Spencer.

    3. Nancy, who married _____ Koon.

The family of George Martin
and his wife
Elizabeth Hoard.

George Martin, third son of Col. Charles and Elizabeth (Burrows) Martin, was born Apr. 6, 1765; died Dec. 19, 1827, near Farmington, W. Va. He resided near Farmington, he married Elizabeth Hoard. She was born June 20, 1768; died June 20, 1854. The children of George and Elizabeth (Hoard) Martin were-

1.   John H., born March 8, 1790; died
                Sept. 24, 1861.

2.   Perry.

3.   Charles.

4.   Malinda.

5.   Elizabeth, married Jesse B. Martin,
                son of Spencer Martin.

6.   William.

7.   Rachael.

8.   Jesse V.

9.   John J.

10. Polly.

The family of Presley Martin
and his wife
Peggy Carter.

Presley Martin, fourth son of Col. Charles and Elizabeth

(Burrows) Martin, resided at New Martinsville, W. Va.

He represented his county in the Legislature of Virginia.

He married Peggy Carter.

Their children were:

1. Marinda.

2. Malinda.

3. Felix.

4. Franklin.

5. Presley.

6. George.

The family of Spencer Martin
and his wife
Polly Snyder.

Spencer Martin, fifth son of Col. Charles and Elizabeth (Burrows) Martin, was born March 6, 1772 at Crooked Run, Monongalia County, W. Va. He died Feb. 13, 1849 near Worthington, W. Va. He resided near Worthington, Marion County, W. Va. He married Polly Snyder (Snider) daughter of John Snyder. She was born Oct. 10, 1774. The children of Spencer and Polly (Snider) were:

1. Dorcas, born Jan. 14, 1794; married John Sturm.

2. Charles, born Sept. 18, 1796; married Elizabeth
      Morgan; moved to Illinois.

3. John S., born March 15, 1801; married Matilda
      Bigler; moved to California.

4. Elizabeth, born Oct. 8, 1798; married Daniel
      Sturm.

5. Jesse B., born Nov. 3, 1802; married Elizabeth
      Martin, daughter of George Martin of
      Buffalo Creek.

6. Spencer, born June 22, 1804; married Sally
      Michael, lived and died in Marion
      County, W. Va.

7. William, born Feb. 17, 1806; married Hannah
      Holbert; moved to Illinois.

8. Margaret, born Oct. 14, 1797.

9. Tobitha, born _____; married John Sturm.

The family of Spencer Martin
and his second wife
Margaret Sturm.

Spencer Martin, son of Col. Charles and Elizabeth
(Burrows) Martin, married second Margaret Sturm, daughter of Jacob and Catherine (Freshour) Sturm. The
children of Spencer Martin and his second wife Margaret
(Sturm) Martin were:

10. Nimrod E., born Jan. 27, 1809; married
     first, Mary Ann Davis; second
     Lavinia Lee.

11. George W., born Jan. 17, 1811; died July
     21, 1875; married Ingaby Sturm.

12. Thornton F., born Nov. 3, 1812; married
     Margaret Nutter; daughter of
     Christopher Nutter.

13. Mary S., born Sept. 23, 1815; married Dennis
     Bruneau of Paris, France.

14. Presley N., born Apr. 23, 1817; married Nancy,
     daughter of Isaac Goosman.

15. Rowley E., born Feb. 27, 1821; died Feb. 1896.
     married Matilda Parish; no issue.

16. Dorsey S., born Apr. 11, 1824; married Rachel
     H., daughter of John H. Martin.

17. Nancy, born Mar. 15, 1827; married Marcus,
     son of Abraham Millan.

18. Matilda C., born Dec. 4, 1836; married Joshua
     C. Parish.

19. Marinda, born Dec. 4, 1831; married William P.
     Fortney.

20. Perry S., born Jan. 29, 1819, died young.

Family Record of Spencer S. Martin, taken from his family
Bible, by his grandson, Felix S. Martin.

Spencer S. Martin was born March 6, 1772.

Mary Snyder, his wife, was born Oct. 10, 1774.

Children:

Dorcas	born	Jan. 17, 1794.		
Charles	"	Sept. 18, 1796.		
Margaret	"	Oct. 14, 1797.		
Elizabeth	"	Oct. 8, 1798.	Married	Daniel Sturm.
John S.	"	Mar. 15, 1801.	"	Matilda ____.
Jesse B.	"	Nov. 3, 1802.	"	Elizabeth ____.
Spencer S.	"	June 22, 1804.	"	Sarah ____.
William	"	Feb. 17, 1806.	"	Ruth ____.
Tobitha	"	-	"	John Sturm.

Married second, Margaret Sturm; their children:

Nimrod E.	born	Jan. 27, 1809.	Married	Mary Ann ____.
Geo. W.	"	Jan. 17, 1811.	"	Ingaby Sturm.
Thornton	"	Nov. 3, 1812.	"	Margaret ____.
Mary S.	"	Sept. 23, 1815.	"	Dennis Bruno.
Presley	"	Apr. 23, 1817.	"	Mary ____.
Perry S.	"	Jan. 29, 1819.	"	-
Rowley E.	"	Feb. 27, 1821.	"	Matilda Parish.
Dorsey S.	"	Apr. 11, 1824.	"	Rachael ____.
Nancy	"	Mar. 15, 1827.	"	Marcus Millan.
Marinda	"	Dec. 4, 1831.	"	Perry Fortney.
Matilda	"	Dec. 4, 1836.	"	Joshua Parrish.

Family Record of Spencer S. Martin, taken from his family
Bible.
Continued.

Jesse B. was the father of Lavena Billingslea, wife of
Morgan Billingslea of Fairmont and of Benj. F. (Hon.)
He is grandfather of Arthur Martin of Fairmont, W. Va.

George W. was the father of my grandfather, Felix S.

Thornton was father of Carson Martin, formerly County
Supt. of Schools, Marion County; also, he is grandfather
of Earl Stuart Morris, Art Editor of the Seattle Intel-
ligencer, Seattle, Wash.

Dorsey S. was father of Amanda, who married Elmer Pigott,
had son Harley, (believe they lived in Shinnston) W. Va.

The family of Ann Martin
and her husband
Richard Harrison.

Ann Martin, daughter of Col. Charles and Elizabeth

(Burrows) Martin, married Richard Harrison.

Their children were:

1. Joseph.

2. Calvin.

3. William.

The family of Elizabeth Martin
and her husband
Norman Randall.

Elizabeth Martin, daughter of Col. Charles and Elizabeth

(Burrows) Martin, married Norman Randall.

The children were:

1. Polly, married _____ Bock.

2. Peggy, married _____ Bock.

3. Betsy, married _____ Bock.

4. William.

5. Hannah, married _____ Conaway.

6. Martin.

7. Millie, married _____ Martin or Monroe.

8. Nancy, married _____ Metz.

The family of Jesse B. Martin
and his wife
Elizabeth Martin.

Jesse B. Martin, son of Spencer and Polly(Snyder)
Martin, was born Nov. 3, 1802; lived on Buffalo Creek,
near Farmington, W. Va. He married Elizabeth Martin,
daughter of George and Elizabeth (Hoard) Martin. Their
children were:

1. Benjamin F., born Oct. 2, 1828; died
   Jan. 20, 1895 at Grafton, W. Va.,
   married Nov. 1854 to Ellen, daughter of James Carlin. No children.

2. Melissa A., born in Elmdale, Kan.; married
   Jacob B. Blackshere.

3. John V., died Sept. 11, 1876.

4. George W., born _____; married Louisa Davis.

5. Elizabeth, married Edward J. Armstrong. No
   children.

6. Laverne Bell, married Morgan Billingslea.
   No children.

7. Winfield Scott.

8. Jesse Thornton, died Jan. 20, 1895; married
   Sophie, daughter of Aaron Morgan.

9. Marion, died young.

10. Belle, married first, James Bussey; second,
    Rev. Williams; lived in Oklahoma.

The family of John V. Martin
and his wife
Sarah Amanda Burdette.

John V. Martin, son of Jesse B. and Elizabeth (Martin) Martin, married Sarah Amanda Burdette. She died Oct. 23, 1908. Their children were:

1. Frederick Thornton, born Feb. 19, 1863; married Mary Gertrude Sinnott.

2. Marion Kate, born Dec. 29, 1864; married Frank C. Fisher.

3. John Franklin, born Sept. 24, 1866; died 1888.

4. Jesse Burrows, born Mar. 1, 1868; married Nancy Amiss.

5. Walter Scott, born Oct. 15, 1869; died Oct. 11, 1871.

6. Elizabeth Broadus, born Mar. 19, 1871; married _____ Abbott.

7. Bernard Leslie, born Apr. 18, 1873; married Lou Sturm.

8. Arthur George, born Oct. 24, 1874; married Mary C. Baker.

The family of Frederick Thornton Martin
and his wife
Mary Gertrude Sinnott.

Frederick Thornton Martin, son of John V. and Sarah
A. (Burdette) Martin, was born Feb. 19, 1863.　　He
married Mary Gertrude Sinnott Oct. 25, 1893.
Their children were:

1.　　John Sinnott, born Oct. 13, 1894.

2.　　Charles Lindsay, born Feb. 1898;
　　　　　　died July 1901.

3.　　James Broadus, born May 7, 1901.

4.　　Mary, born Sept. 10, 1903.

The family of George W. Martin
and his wife
Louisa Davis.

George W. Martin, son of Jesse B. and Elizabeth
(Martin) Martin, married Louisa Davis, daughter of
Marcene Davis. The children of George W. and Louisa
(Davis) Martin were:

1.   William.

2.   Ida, married _____ Hyde.

3.   Flora, married _____ Brown.

Dr. Winfield Scott Martin.

Dr. Winfield Scott Martin, son of Jesse B. and Elizabeth (Martin) Martin, married first Clara Sinsel. There were no survivors. He married second, Laura Startzman.

Their children were:

1. Forest.

2. Wilson B.

3. Carl.

The family of Jesse Thornton Martin
and his wife
Sophia L. Morgan.

Jesse Thornton Martin, son of Jesse B. and Elizabeth (Martin) Martin, was born in Marion Co., W. Va. He died June 1911. He married Sophia L. Morgan, 1864 in Penn. She was the daughter of Aaron and Rebecca (Cochran) Morgan. She was born Nov. 10, 1845, in Marion County, W. Va.; died March 6, 1929. Their children, born in Kansas, were:

1. Porter W., born 1868; married Sept. 21, 1893, Leila J. Burns, daughter of James H. and Mary D. (Kyle) Burns.

2. Harry Lee, born Aug. 12, 1872; died Sept. 7, 1902.

The family of Porter W. Martin
and his wife
Leila J. Burns.

Porter W. Martin, son of Jesse Thornton and Sophia
L. (Morgan) Martin, was born 1868. He married Lelia
J. Burns, Sept. 21, 1893. She was the daughter of
James H. and Mary D. (Kyle) Burns. She was born in
1867 in Botetourt County, Va.   Their dhild was:

1.   Hugh Burns, born Dec. 21, 1898,
        in Marion County.

Charles Martin.

Charles Martin, son of Spencer and Polly (Snyder)
Martin, was born Sept. 18, 1796; moved to Illinois
and died there. He married Elizabeth Morgan.
Their children were:

1. Mary.
2. Perry.

James Daugherty (Dougherty).

Fairfax Grant to James and John Daugherty (Dougherty)
Aug. 9, 1766. 400 acres adjoining land of Thomas Dent,
Frederick County, Va.

In 1778 James and John Daugherty were both living in
Monongalia County, Va.
James Daugherty served as Captain in the McIntosh campaign
1778. (Ref.: On file in Washington. "Captain Dougherty
appears on a return of officers and privates from the county
of Monongalia, for the Expedition to the "Indian Country".
The return was not dated. Endorsement shows, "Officers under
Col. Thomas Gaddis for the Indian Expedition in 1778 against
the Indian towns west of the Ohio, which lasted three months."

The Chief Clerk states that the only reason for this card
was that when the company of 349 men were drafted for the
Expedition that twelve men from Captain Daugherty's company
were drafted to complete the company.
History of Monongalia Co. by Wiley, page 486; John Evans served as Lieut. Col., James Daugherty served as Captain, Richard
Tennant as drummer, Peter Haught and James Snodgrass as private's in McIntosh's Campaign 1778. These names were secured
from affidavits made Nov. 15, 1811, before the county court,
by John Evans and David Scott, and later, by Richard Tenant

and Peter Haught. The muster roll was destroyed in the
burning of the clerks office in 1796.

The original tax records in Charleston, W. Va. show that
there was but one James Daugherty living near Morgantown
from 1776 through 1803, and one Enos Daugherty, who was
the physician.

In George Washington's Diary, Vol. II, the General speaks
of spending the night in the home of James Daugherty in
Monongalia County, mentioning that it was just a "tolerable
home".

Sept. 9, 1785 James Daugherty purchased 3 lots from Zackwell
Morgan. (Recorded in Morgantown Court House.)
In 1789 James Daugherty was County Commissioner.

A deed made in 1799 (recorded in Morgantown Court House)
by James Daugherty and his wife Susannah _____.

Will dated Nov. 24, 1804 mentions only his son, Enos.

James Daugherty, Cont'd.

The children of James and Susannah _____ Daugherty were:

1.   Enos, born ca 1763; died Feb. 10, 1826
   in Morgantown; married Jean
   Crampton, born March 2, 1767.
   Their children were:
   a.   Joseph.
   b.   James.
   c.   Susan.
   d.   Anna.

   Enos Daugherty was a director in the
   first bank in Morgantown (1814). He
   was said to have been the first resident physician practicing in 1805,
   aged about 40.

2.   Elizabeth, born ca 1767; married ca 1785
   Judge John Collins of Pennsylvania.
   Morgantown and Portsmouth, Ohio.
   He was born Sept. 7, 1765 in Pa.;
   died Aug. 16, 1842 in Portsmouth,
   Ohio. Their children were:

   a.   Cynthia, born Mar. 10, 1787
   in Monongalia Co., Va.; married Sept. 5, 1803, Capt.
   Moses Fuqua.
   b.   Polly (Mary) born Jan. 16,
   1791 in Va. married William
   Robey.
   c.   Nancy, married William Young.
   d.   Amelia, married Phillip Moore.
   e.   Thomas, married Susannah Waller.
   f.   John.
   g.   Enos.

   Judge John Collins married second, Jane
   Lamson. Their children were: Elizabeth,
   Susan, Joseph, William and David.

3.   Amelia, born 1770; died 1824; married Col. James
   Scott of Monongalia County, Va. For
   their children, see next page.

The family of James Scott
and his wife
Amelia Daugherty.

James Scott, son of Captain David Scott and his wife

Judith (Cunningham) Scott, was born 1765 in Virginia

died July 5, 1848 near Morgantown, Monongalia County,

W. Va. He served in the Revolutionary War as a musi-

cian, at the age of 13. He received a pension (see

Virginia Pension list, page 17; also State of Virginia

Library Report, page 392. For Military services in

the War of 1812, see "History of the Panhandle of W. Va."

published in 1879, page 319. He served as Colonel in

this war). He married Amelia Daugherty, daughter of

Captain James Daugherty of Monongalia Co., W. Va.

Amelia Daugherty died near Morgantown July 7, 1824.

The children of James and Amelia (Daugherty) Scott were:

1. Theresa, called Terray, was born 1789;
         married John Shively, Sept. 26,
         1809. They lived in Marion, Ind.

2. David, born 1791, died 1875; married Marjory
         Harrison, daughter of Richard Har-
         rison, Jr. Some of their children
         were: Jesse, Jehu, John, Joseph,
         Richard and Elizabeth, who married
         Thomas Pindall. (See sketch of
         Pindall family).
         Richard Harrison, Jr. married
         Nancy Martin, daughter of Col.
         Charles and Elizabeth (Burrows)
         Martin. (see sketch of the Martin
         family).

3. Matilda, born 1793; married Thomas Hess in
         Aug. 1812. Lived in Henry Co., Ind.

The family of James Scott
and his wife
Amelia Daugherty.

Continued.

4.   William T., born Nov. 5, 1795; died Mar.18,
         1862; married Juliet Marchand;
         lived in Alexandria.

5.   Enos. D., born 1799; died Jan. 21, 1865, age
         66 yrs., 8 mo., 26 days. Unmarried.

6.   Juliet, born Feb. 16, 1803; died Feb. 5, 1874;
         married John Hamilton, son of Thomas
         and Elizabeth (Fickel) Hamilton of
         Monongalia Co., W. Va. John and
         Juliet Hamilton lived in Perry Co.,
         Ohio. (For children see Hamilton).

7.   Bushrod W., born 1808; married Apr. 4, 1826
         to Henrietta Clark, daughter of
         Josiah Clark; married second, Lucy
         Chapman. He died Aug. 1871.

8.   Sanford B., born 1812; married Hannah Tibbs,
         Nov. 19, 1835. They lived in Ind.

9.   Rawley, married Christina Stealey, said to
         have gone to New York City. Christina
         Stealey was the daughter of John and
         Prudence (Cozad) Stealey. John Stealey
         came from Maryland, died in Jefferson-
         ville, Ind. Prudence Cozad Stealey
         died Aug. 18, 1822 aged 60. Their
         children were: Sarah, who married
         Jacob Kiger., Elizabeth who married
         Cornelius Berkshire, Christena who
         married Rawley Scott, Catherine who
         married first, Col. Richard Watts;
         second, William Hart.

10.   Dorsey, married near St. Louis, Mo. Went to
         Scott County, Ind.

11.   Caroline, married first, Ishmael Massie, 1835;
         married second, Alexander Smith Menefee.
         No children by either marriage.

                    The family of Julia (Juliet) Scott
                           and her husband
                           John Hamilton.

Julia Scott, daughter of James and Amelia (Daugherty) Scott,

was born in Monongalia County, Va. on Feb. 16, 1803. She mar-

ried John Hamilton of the same county, Nov. 4, 1824. He was

the son of Thomas and Elizabeth (Fickel) Hamilton of Monongalia

County, W. Va. John Hamilton was born May 19, 1801; died Feb.

27, 1883. Both are buried in Rehoboth Cemetery, Perry County,

Ohio. Julia Scott Hamilton died Feb. 5, 1874. Their children were:

1.   Salathial, born Nov. 5, 1825 in Virginia; died in
            Roseburg, Oregon.

2.   Francis Marion, born 1827 in Virginia; died in Illinois.

3.   Sanford S., born in Ohio, married Harriet Cooper.
            (Born in 1829)

4.   James Thomas, born in Ohio in 1831, died at the age
            of 22 years, unmarried.

5.   Caroline, born March 10, 1833; married in Perry Co.,
            Ohio, to Rev. Asbury Clarke Kelley, a
            Methodist Minister. They were married
            March 10, 1853.

6.   Martha, born in Ohio in 1836; married _____ Dean.

7.   Jane, born in Perry Co., Ohio, Nov. 14, 1838, mar-
            ried William Lyons; died Jan. 20, 1911.

8.   Elizabeth, born in Perry Co., Ohio, in 1841; mar-
            ried John Pace; died in 1912. Their
            children:
            Charles Pace and Homer Pace, both of
            whom live (1938) in New York City.

9.   Emma, born in Perry Co., Ohio, 1843; married
            _____ Shelahammer.

The family of Caroline Hamilton
and her husband
Reverend Asbury Clarke Kelley.

Caroline Hamilton, daughter of John Hamilton and his
wife, Julia (Scott) Hamilton, was born in Perry Co.,
Ohio, March 10, 1833; married March 10, 1853 to Rev.
Asbury Clarke Kelley of Perry Co. (son of James and
Elizabeth Shaw Kelley of Fauquier Co., Va., later of
Perry Co., Ohio); was a descendant of James Claypoole
of Philadelphia. Their children were:

1.   Laura Jane, born Dec. 20, 1853 in New
            Lexington, Perry Co., Ohio.

2.   Martha Maria, born Feb. 18, 1856 in
            Barlow, Ohio.

3.   Carrie May, born Feb. 20, 1864, in
            Ironton, Ohio.

Caroline (Hamilton) Kelley died April 21, 1915. Rev.
Asbury Clarke Kelley died April 15, 1907. Both are
buried in Green Lawn Cemetery, Columbus, Ohio.

The family of John Hamilton
and his wife
Martha _____.

John Hamilton, born ca 1730; died before 1804; married Martha ____. Had land in Tygarts Valley; was appointed Captain of Augusta Co., Militia. In 1782 census for Monongalia Co., is listed as having five in the family. Feb. 18, 1784 had 400 acres of land on Beaver Creek; 400 acres on Scotts Run to complete his settlement 1773. He also had land in Kentucky.

Recorded in Book 7, page 111., also deed book M, page 557. Virginia State Land Grant Office.

The children of John and Martha ____ Hamilton were:

1. Sarah, who married Benjamin Leggett.

2. Catherine, who married Frederick Zimmerman March 14, 1803.

3. Nancy, who married Moses Musgrave; came to Coshocton Co., Ohio. They were married in 1796 in Virginia.

4. Elizabeth, who married George Jones?

5. Thomas, who married about 1799 to Elizabeth Fickel, daughter of Joseph, Sr., and Elizabeth (____) Fickel.

6. George, who died single. (Died in Monongalia County).

The family of Thomas Hamilton
and his wife
Elizabeth Fickel.

Thomas Hamilton, son of John and Martha (_____)

Hamilton, was born in Monongalia County, Va., about

1775-8. His will was probated in that county Nov.

1842. He married Elizabeth Fickel, daughter of Joseph

and Elizabeth (_____) Fickel. Their children were:

1. John, born May 19, 1801; died Feb. 27, 1883;
   married Nov. 4, 1824, Julia Scott,
   daughter of James and Amelia Daugherty Scott. For their children see
   preceding page.

2. A daughter, who married James Brewer.

3. Elizabeth, who married John Knotts. (Knott)
   July 29, 1823.

4. Joseph, born ca 1808; married in 1833, in
   Perry Co., Ohio, to Sarah Weirick.

5. Gilly, married Dec. 16, 1838 to Charles Pace.
   (William Johnson swears she is over
   18).

6. Martha, married March 4, 1840 to William
   Johnson by S. Curran, J. P.

7. Thomas J., a physician in New Lexington, Ohio;
   was born 1812; died 1873; married
   Mary Morrow May 7, 1841. Their children were: Two, who died in infancy;
   two daughters lived whose names are
   unknown. Mary, wife of Thomas J.
   died 1851; buried in the Methodist
   Cemetery in New Lexington. Also buried
   on the Hamilton lot are the infant
   children.

8. William, born 1816; died in 1874; married in 1844
   to Hester Ann (Donley)? Their children
   were:
   a. Thomas
   b. Henry
   c. Martha, who married Wm. England.

The family of Thomas Hamilton, Cont'd.

        d.   Ann.
        e.   Caroline.

        William was buried in the Methodist
        Church Cemetery, New Lexington, Ohio.

9.   Zilpha, in 1850 was living in the home of Gilah
        Pace., Rehobeth, Perry Co., Ohio.

Deed book A, page 96.
New Lexington, Perry Co., Ohio.

This indenture made this second day of June in the
year of our Lord 1818 between Thomas Hamilton of Monongalia County and State of Virginia of the one part and
Daniel Fickle of Perry County and State of Ohio of the
other part witnesseth that the said Thomas Hamilton for
and in consideration of the sum of $100 current money
of the U. S. to him in hand paid the receipt whereof
he doth hereby acknowledge and forever acquit and dis-
charge the said Daniel Fickle his executors and administrators hath granted, bargained and sold and confirmed
and by these presents also grant bargain sell and confirm
unto the said Daniel Fickle his heirs and assigns forever
all the tenth part or parcel of land, the whole of which
contains 160 acres of land being the northeast quarter of
section number 36 of Township number 17, of Range number
16 which said 160 acres of land belonged to the deceased
Joseph Fickle, Sr., of Fairfield County, State of Ohio;
together with all improvements, water courses and etc.,
whatsoever to the said premises belonging or in anywise
pertaining and the reversions, remainder and profits
thereof with all of the aforesaid tenth part of the estate
right, title, interest, property claim and demand of the
said Thomas Hamilton and to the   to have and to hold
the lands hereby conveyed the full tenth share of the
aforementioned premises and with the appertances unto the

said Daniel Fickle his heirs and assigns forever to the
only proper use and behalf of him the said Daniel his
heirs and assigns and the said Thomas Hamilton for him-
self his heirs, executors and administrators do coven-
ant want promise and agree to the said Daniel Fickle,
his heirs and etc., that the premises before mentioned
now are and forever hereafter shall remain free of and
from others and forever gives, grants, bargains, sells
the dower now at present belonging to Widow Elizabeth
Fickle, mother of said Hamilton's wife and Daniel her
life time excepted, likewise judgments, executions, titles,
troubles, charges and incumbrances whatsoever done or suf-
fered to be done by him, the said Thomas Hamilton and the
said Thomas Hamilton and his heirs all and singular the
premises hereby bargained and sold with appertances unto
the said Daniel Fickle his heirs and assigns against him the
said Thomas Hamilton and his heirs.

In witness whereof the said Thomas Hamilton has hereunto set his hand and seal the day and year above written.

Thomas Hamilton

Elizabeth   (her mark)

Signed in the presence of us

We, James Tibbs and James Barker, Justices of the Peace
and for the County of Monongalia in the State of Virginia do
certify that Elizabeth Hamilton, wife of Thomas Hamilton
parties to the written conveyance personally appears before

us in our County and after having the deed fully explained to her, she the said Elizabeth Hamilton said she acknowledged the same freely and voluntarily of her own will without the persuasion of her husband and that she wished not to retract it, given under our hands this second day of June 1818.

Michael Fickel

In "Pennsylvania German Pioneers" by Strasburger and
Hinke, Vol. 2, page 143, List 37A of the passengers
on board the ship Hope Gallery, Daniel Reidt, Commander,
Sept. 23, 1734, is mentioned Michael Fikel, aged 25.
Also mentioned in Prof. I Rupps "Thirty thousand Im-
migrants", Page 97.
Note:

   This name is spelled, Van Fikel, Fickel, Fickle.

   They came to this country from Holland.

Department of
Internal Affairs
Harrisburg, Pa.
Warrent F#7

Pennsylvania by the Proprietaries.
Whereas Michael Fickel of the County
of Lancaster hath requested that we
would grant him to take up one hundred acres of land situated in Stras-
burg township whereon he has been
about twelve months settled and
adjoining to Thomas Green and Matthias Slaymaker in the said county
of Lancaster for which he agrees to
pay to our use the sum of fifteen
pounds ten shillings current money of
this Province for ye said hundred acres
and the yearly quit rent of one-half
penny Sterling for every acre thereof.
   These are therefore to authorize

to be surveyed unto the said Michael
Fickel at the place aforesaid according to the method of townships appointed
the said quantity of one hundred acres
if not already surveyed or appropriated
and make return thereof unto the Sec-
retary's Office in order for further
confirmation for which this shall be
thy sufficient warrent.

Which survey in case the said Michael
Fickel fulfil the above agreement with-
in six months from date hereof shall be
valid otherwise void.

Given under my hand and the lesser
seal of our Province at Philadelphia
this twenty-eighth day of April Anno
Dom. 1736.

Tho. Penn.

To Benjamin Eastburn Surveyor General.

Patent book P. 56
Page 67.

The Commonwealth of Pennsylvania.
To all to whom these presents shall
come Greeting. Know ye that in consideration on the monies paid by
Michael Fickel unto the late Proprietaries, into the Receiver General's

Office of this Commonwealth at the
granting of the warrent herein after
mentioned and of the sum of two hundred and twenty-five dollars and
twenty-eight cents lawful money, now
paid by Balsor Barkman into the Rec-
civer General's Office of this Commonwealth, there is granted by the
said Commonwealth unto the said Balsor Barkman a certain tract of land
called "Brandiwine" situated in Stras-
burg township Lancaster County beginning at a stone thence by land of
Thomas Green and land of John Huston
South thirteen degrees East one hundred and thirteen perches to a chest-
nut stump thence by land of Colen
Brown and land of Thomas Hastings
South eighty-seven degrees West
one hundred and sixty-eight perches to
a post thence by said Hastings land
and land of Matthias Slaymaker North
one hundred and nineteen perches to
a post and thence by land of the
London Company East one hundred
and forty-two perches to the beginning containing one hundred and

five acres and the allowance of six
per cent for roads &c. Which said
tract was surveyed in pursuance of
a warrent dated the twenty-eighth
day of April 1736, granted to the
said Michael Fickel whose right therein by virtue of sundry good convey-
ances and assurances in the law duly
had and executed became vested in the
said Balsor Barkman with the appurt-
ences. To have and to hold the said
tract or parcel of land with the appertances unto the said Balsor Barkman
his heirs and assigns forever. Free
and clear of all restrictions and re-
servations as to mines royalties quit
rents or otherwise excepting and re-
serving only the fifth part of all
gold and Silver ore for the use of
this Commonwealth to be delivered at
the pits mouth clear of all charges.
In witness whereof Thomas McKean
Governor of the said Commonwealth
hath hereto set his hand and caused
the State Seal to be hereunto affixed the seventh day of September in the

year of our Lord one thousand eight
hundred and five and of the Commonwealth the twenty-ninth.

Inrolled II September 1805.

Michael Fickel purchased land in Frederick County, Maryland,
recorded in Frederick County as follows:

Deed   Recorded May 16, 1763. Between Robert Miller
Book H
P. 440   and Michael Fickel. The land Michael purchased

            was referred to as "The addition to Brooks

            Discovery on the Richlands".

Book J   Recorded Nov. 22, 1764. Between Michael Fickel
P. 992
            and Richard Brook.

Book K   May 7, 1766. Between John Hager of Frederick
P. 479
            and Michael Fickel.

Last Will and Testament
of
Michael Fickel.

In the Name of God Amen:

The twentieth day of November in the year of our
Lord Seventeen Hundred and Seventy, I, Michael Fickle,
of Frederick County in the Province of Maryland, Farmer
being very sick and wek of body but of perfect mind and
memory thanks be given unto God, therefore calling unto
mind the mortality of my Body and knowing that it is
appointed for all men once to die, do make and ordain
this my last Will and Textament that is to say:

Principally and first of all I give and recommend
my Soul into the Hands of God that gave it, and for my
Body I recommend it to the earth to be buried in a
Christian like and decent manner at the discretion of
my Executor, nothing doubting but at the general Resurrection I shall receive the same again by the mighty
power of God and as touching such worldly estate where
with it hath pleased God to bless me in this life. I
give, devise and dispose of the same in the following
manner and form, Imprimis, I give and bequeath unto
Margaret my beloved wife one-third part of my whole
estate, Real and personal; Goods and Chattles; Rights
and Credits; and over and above that said third part one
horse and two cows to be at her own choice to her, her
heirs and assigns forever. Item, my will further is and

Last Will and Testament
of
Michael Fickel

Continued.

I do appoint that all the residue of my whole estate
as above (saving to my said wife, her part as above
mentioned) be sold and the amount arising from the
appraisement of my Goods and Chattels; Rights and
Credits; and the sale of my land and crop in the
ground (saving to my said wife, her third part thereof be disposed of in the following manner, that is to
say, that my just debts be first paid thereoutof and
that my beloved son, Joseph shall be paid for what
improvements he hath made on my plantation bought
from William Wells according to the estimation of two
reputable persons indifferently chosen by my said wife
and son Joseph for that purpose, and then that my beloved daughter Elizabeth shall be paid the sum of ten
pounds money, which I do hereby give and bequeath to
her, her heirs and assigns forever and then that the
residue or remainder of the above amount shall be equally divided among my eleven children hereinafter named
Viz: Gabriel, Mary, Joseph, Matthias, Daniel, Benjamin,
Isaac, Jonathan, Esther, Naomi and Rachel, which several
and respective parts I do hereby give and bequeath unto my beloved eleven children above named, respectively
to them their heirs and assigns forever excepting that
in case any of my said children that are under age which
should be called away by death before they are of age to re-

Last Will and Testament
of
Michael Fickel.

Continued.

ceive their legacies such legacy or legacies shall be
equally divided amongst the surviving part of my eleven
children as aforesaid and further my will is and I do
appoint that my five youngest children, Benjamin, Isaac,
Jonathan, Naomi and Rachel shall dwell with their mother
until they are of age and that their respective legacies
shall be put out at use with sufficient securities by
my Executors hereinafter named and that the amount of
the interest arising therefrom shall be paid yearly and
every year to my wife to enable her to bring up and edu-
cate my children in a Christian like manner. And further
I do will and appoint that the Executor of this my last
Will and Testament shall sell all of my land (not bequeathed to my wife) immediately after my decease as
soon as an opportunity may appear to sell to the best
advantage and I do hereby authorize, appoint and empower
my Executor to make good and sufficient conveyance and
right thereto. And lastly I do hereby constitute make
and ordain my son Joseph above named, my only and soul
Executor of this my last Will and Testament.

And I do hereby utterly disallow revoke, disannull
all and every other former Testaments, Wills, legacies,
and Executors by me in any way before this time named,
Willed and bequeathed Ratifying and confirming this and

Last Will and Testament
of
Michael Fickel.

Continued.

no other to be my last Will and Testament in witness
whereof I have hereunto set my hand and seal the day
and year above written.

Michael Fickel   (Seal)

Signed, sealed, published and declared by the said
Michael Fickel as his last Will and Testament in the
presence of us the subscribers.

Samuel McFenan   Benjamin Paddin

Wm. Blair

On the third day of January 1771, came Samuel McFenan
and Benjamin Paddin two of the subscribing witnesses
to the aforegoing Will and made oath on the Holy Evan-
gels of Almighty God that they did see the Testator
Michael Fickel sign and seal the said Will and heard
him publish, pronounce and declare the same to be his
last Will and Testament and that at the time of his so
doing he was to the best of their apprehension of a
sound and disposing mind and memory and that they also
did see William Blair, the other subscribing witness
sign his name as a witness thereto in the presence of
each other and in the presence of the Testator.

Sworn before F. Bowles Dy   Cozy.

Last Will and Testament
of
Margaret Fickel.

In The Name of God Amen.

I, Margaret Fickle of Frederick County, and the
State of Maryland, being in perfect health of Body
and of sound and disposing mind and memory, but calling unto mind the mortality of my Body and knowing
that it is appointed for all men once to die do make
and ordain this my last Will and Testament. That is
to say,

First and principally I recommend my soul to
Almighty God that gave it and my Body to the earth to
be buried in a decent Christian Buriel at the discretion
of my Executors nothing doubting but at the General
Resurrection I shall receive the same again and as
touching such worldly estate wherewith it hath pleased
God to bless me in this life, I give, devise and dispose of in the manner following:

Imprimis: I give and bequeath to my daughter Rachel
all part of my land that lays on the north side of Piney
Creek (Viz: that side of Piney Creek whereon she now dwells)
to be enjoyed by her, and her heirs and assigns forever.

Item. My will and intention is that all the remainder
of my land (Viz) all that part that lays on the South side
of Piney Creek whereon I now dwell shall be sold at public vendure by my Executors hereafter named, who I do hereby

Last Will and Testament
of
Margaret Fickle.

Continued.

authorize and empower to give to the purchaser or
purchasers as good a deed of conveyance as I myself
now do and to divide all the money arising from the
sale thereof equally between my son Gabriel Fickle,
my daughter, Mary Dun, my daughter Elizabeth Williams,
my son Joseph Fickle, my son Matthias Fickle, my daughter Esther Wilson, my son Benjamin Fickle, my daughter Naomi Baldwin, my son Isaac Fickle, and grandchild
Mary Fickle, daughter of my son Jonathan, deceased.
Lastly I do hereby constitute and appoint my trusty
friend Elijah Baldwin and my son-in-law Daniel Baldwin
sole Executors of this my last Will and Testament and
I do hereby utterly disallow, revoke and disannull
all other Will or Wills by me heretofore made ratifying and confirming this to be my last Will and Testament in witness whereof I have hereunto set my hand and
seal this ninth day of January, Seventeen hundred and
Ninety-Four.

her
Margaret X Fickle (Seal)
mark.

Signed, sealed, published, pronounced, and delivered
by the said Margaret Fickle as her last Will and Testament in the presence of us who in her presence and in
the presence of each other have hereunto subscribed

Last Will and Testament
of
Margaret Fickle.

Continued.

our hands.

Robert Jamison

Henry Spalding

Francis Elder   (Frederick)

Frederick County, April 3, 1795, then came Elijah Baldwin
and Daniel Baldwin and made oath that the aforegoing in-
strument of writing is the true and whole last Will and
Testament of Margaret Fickle late of Frederick Co. deceased,
that hath come to their hands and possession and that they
do not know of any other.

Geo. Murdock.   Register.

Frederick County, April 3, 1795, then came Robert Jamison and
Francis Elder two of the subscribing witnesses to the aforegoing last Will and Testament of Margaret Fickle, late of
Frederick County, deceased, and made oath on the Holy Evan-
gels of Almighty God, that they did see the Testator therein named sign and seal this Will that they heard her publish,
pronounce and declare the same to be her last Will and Testament that at the time of her so doing she was to the best of
their apprehension of sound and disposing mind, memory and
understanding that they respectively subscribed their names as
Witnesses to this Will in the presence of and at the request of

Last Will and Testament
of
Margaret Fickle.

Continued.

the Testator and that they did also see Henry Spalding,

the other subscribing witness sign his name as a witness

thereto in the presence of and at the request of the

Testator and all in the presence of each other.

George Murdock.   Register.

                    The family of Michael Fickel
                         and his wife
                    Margaret _____

The children of Michael and Margaret _____ Fickel

as recorded in his will were:

1.   Gabriel, who had land in York County, Pa.
                was on tax list 1780-1782.

2.   Joseph, born ca 1750; died in Fairfield
                Co., Ohio, about 1814. Married
                Elizabeth _____.

3.   Mary, married _____ Dunn.

4.   Matthias, was living in Frederick County,
                Md., in 1796.

5.   Daniel, born ca 1756; Served in Rev. War.
                (see Pa. Archives Vol. 5, Series
                5, page 92. Class Roll Capt.
                George Ensole's Co. Province
                (c) first class, Daniel Fickle,
                1781.

6.   Benjamin, Lieut. Md. Continental Line; ser-
                ved three years (Archives of Md.)
                Went to Ohio in 1804. Married
                Phoebe _____. Buried in Pike Twp.
                Coshocton Co., Ohio.

7.   Isaac, served in the Rev. War from Talbot Co.,
                Maryland 1781. (Archives of Md. Vol.
                18, page 408.)

8.   Jonathan, died before 1794. Left daughter, Mary.

9.   Esther, born 1752; died 1840. Married William
                Wilson, Rev. Sold. (See Roster of
                Rev. Sold. buried in Ohio).

10.   Naomi, married Daniel Baldwin. Their children:
                a. Mary.
                b. Kezia
                c. Hester, married Samuel Hutchinson.
                d. Rachael, married Phillip Miller.
                e. Abby, married Jacob Crouse.
                f. Margaret Naomi, married David Flegel.
                g. Elizabeth, married George Flegel.
                h. Jesse.
                i. John.
                j. Isaac.

The family of Michael Fickel
and his wife
Margaret _____

Continued.

              k.   Elige (Elijah).
              l.   Daniel.

11. Elizabeth, married _____ Williams.

12. Rachel, died ca 1830, unmarried. Her will
            filed in Frederick County mentions
            only a niece, Mary, wife of John
            Stitely, to whom she leaves the
            land she inherited from her mother,
            Margaret Fickel.

Abstract of the will of Daniel Baldwin.

No mention of his wife, it is inferred she had died previous to July 11, 1823 when he signed his will. Mentions children named on a preceding page and three grandchildren, namely,

> John Shoemaker.
> Agnes Shoemaker.
> Stephen Shoemaker.

Witnesses to will:

> Michael Null.
> Jacob Feeser.
> Abraham Crouse.

Pension Application of Benjamin Fickle.

Coshocton County.

Lieut. Contl. Md. served three years, ten months,
residence Frederick Co., Maryland; married Phebe
(died before 1857), children: one was Isaac, living in Williams Co., Ohio, in 1857, left eight
children, three living in 1857; Rachel Vansky
(Vanscoy), Catherine Kilpatrick and Isaac H. Fickle;
soldier died May 20, 1839 leaving widow; in March
1822 appeared before J. P. in Muskingum Co., Ohio;
Dec. 27, 1833 certified his service in Coshocton Co.,
(Pike Twp.), Ohio for increase pay; pension last
paid to Sept. 4, 1838, Treas. Ref. S 8478 Md.

Pa. Archives Vol. 7, Series 5.
6th, company of Flying Camp 1776 first battalion of
the Flying Camp of Lancaster Co., Pa. under Col. James
Cunningham.

From Maryland Hist. Mag. Vol. 22 Sept. 1927 No. 3.

Daniel and Benjamin Fickel enlisted July 1,
1775 in Capt. Thomas Price's company of
Riflemen of the United Colonies. They
marched to Boston.

Muskingum Co., Ohio, Deed Book G, Page 443 - 785

U. S. to Benjamin Fickle assignee of Benjamin Twiner land
grant 1812. Recorded July 1, 1822. Seal of the Land Office R. P. 560 Vol. 3, Rev. Sold.

Deed book J, page 242
Lancaster, Fairfield County, Ohio.

Indenture made the first day of December in the year
1814 between Joseph Fickel of Muskingum County and
State of Ohio of the one part and Daniel Fickel of
Fairfield County, State of Ohio of the other part.
Witnesseth that the said Joseph Fickel for and in
consideration of the sum of $100 current money of
U. S. to him in hand paid the receipt whereof he
doth hereby acknowledge and forever acquit and dis-
charge the said Daniel Fickel and his heirs and etc.
Northeast quarter Section 36, Township 17, Range 16
which said 160 acres, land belonged to the late
Joseph Fickel, Sr., of Fairfield County. The dower
now belonging to Widow Elizabeth Fickel, mother of
Joseph and Daniel.

                              Joseph Fickel
                              Mary Fickel

The family of Joseph Fickel
and his wife
Elizabeth _____.

Joseph Fickel, son of Michael and Margaret _____ Fickel,
was born ca 1750; went to Ohio in 1804; purchased 160
acres of land in Fairfield County (now Perry) in military district Section 36, Township 17, Range 16, in 1812.
U. S. Patent March 5. He married Elizabeth _____. He
died in 1813. The children of Joseph and Elizabeth _____
Fickel as mentioned in Book A, Court House, New Lexington,
Perry County, Ohio, were:

1. Daniel, who married "Hetty" Tipton (or
        Lipton) Aug. 1, 1815 in Mus-
        kingum County, Ohio.

2. Joseph Jr., who married Oct. 1, 1805 Mary
        Dusenberry, daughter of William
        Dusenberry (See Dusenberry family)

3. Elizabeth, born ca 1788, married Thomas
        Hamilton of Monongalia Co., W. Va.
        (See Hamilton family).

4. William, who married Ann _____.

5. Jonathan, who married in 1817 in Fairfield
        Co., Rhoda Skinner, daughter of
        Robert and Elizabeth (Spencer)
        Skinner. (See family of Rhoda Skinner).

6. Benjamin, who married Oct. 3, 1805, Rebecca
        Dusenberry, daughter of William
        Dusenberry.

7. Rachel, who married Edward Hamilton in Monon-
        galia County, W. Va.

8. Edward, who married Rebecca _____.

9. Isaac, who married Mary Fate (Tate) in 1816 in
        Fairfield Co., Ohio.

10. Sarah, who married George Crosson in 1812 in
        Fairfield Co., Ohio.

The family of Joseph Fickel.

Continued.

All of these children sold their share of the 160 acres to Daniel, apparently the oldest brother. Elizabeth, the mother, was living and had her dower right.

All deeds were dated 1818 and referred to land in military district Section 36, Township 17, Range 16, belonging to the late Joseph Fickel, head of the family in Perry County, Ohio.

Daniel Fickel and his wife, Hetty, sold this land to John Burkey, Oct. 12, 1818.

The family of Joseph D. Fickel
and his wife
Mary Dusenberry.

Joseph D. Fickel was born 1779: died Nov. 6, 1850;

married Oct. 1, 1805 to Mary Dusenberry; born June

3, 1783, died April 2, 1860. Both buried in Bethel

Cemetery near the village of Sego, Perry County, Ohio.

Their children were:

1. Sarah, who married _____ Barnet.

2. Elizabeth, who married _____ Weirick.

3. John.

4. Catherine, who married Abraham Bowser.

5. Rebecca, who married Nov. 3, 1836 to
         Wesley Davis.

6. Mary, who married Oct. 29, 1835 to
         Jacob Bowman.

7. Josiah.

8. William, who was deceased in 1860; left
         three children namely:
              William.
              Sarah.
              Elizabeth Hull.

9. Henry, born Oct. 12, 1812; died 1852;
         married Apr. 17, 1834 to Dolly
         Robey. Their children were:
         a. Sarah Elizabeth, born Feb.
            1, 1835.
         b. Thomas Vanire, born Feb.
            12, 1837.
         c. Joseph Allen, born Apr. 6,
            1839.
         d. Nancy Jane, born July 10, 1841.
         e. Mary, born Oct. 15, 1844.
         f. Catherine, born Jan. 28, 1847.
         g. Abraham, born Dec. 7, 1850.

The family of Benjamin Fickel
and his wife
Rebecca Dusenberry.

Benjamin Fickel, son of Joseph and Elizabeth (_____)
Fickel, married Oct. 3, 1805, Rebecca Dusenberry,
daughter of William and Elizabeth _____ Dusenberry.
The children of Benjamin and Rebecca (Dusenberry)
Fickel were:

1. William (eldest son).

2. Jane.

3. Joseph.

4. Isaac.

5. Samuel.

6. Washington.

7. Benjamin.

8. Jacob, married Catherine Craig. Their
   children were: Mary Jane,
   who married Isaac Guthrie;
   Rebecca Catherine, Amanda,
   Elizabeth (all unmarried),
   Nancy, who married P. P.
   Gardner, William F., who
   married Zoe Corwin. Henry Clay
   Fickel, who married Elizabeth
   Garbison.

9. Silas.

10. Nancy, who married George Robey; moved to
    Morrow Co., Ohio. Their children
    were: Rebecca, Sarah H., Thomas B.
    and Dortha H. George Robey and
    Nancy Fickel were married Dec.
    17, 1840. Nancy died and he mar-
    ried again.

11. Mary Ann, who married Wm. R. House, Mar. 2,
    1837.

12. Sarah, who married Jacob Younkin, Oct. 7, 1843.

The family of Jonathan Fickel
and his wife
Rhoda Skinner.

Jonathan Fickel, son of Joseph and Elizabeth _____ Fickel, married, March 26, 1817 in Fairfield County, Ohio, Rhoda Skinner, daughter of Robert and Elizabeth (Spencer) Skinner (see family of Rhoda Skinner); lived in Perry County, Ohio, until 1841 when they moved to Franklin County, Ohio. The children of Jonathan and Rhoda (Skinner) Fickel were:

1. Rebecca, who married _____ Latham.

2. Mary, who married _____ Armstrong.

3. Betty, who married _____ Skinner.

4. Sarah, who married John Bowser.

5. Eliza, who married _____ Bailey.

6. Nelson.

7. Alfred.

8. William, who married Virginia _____.

9. Robert.

10. George.

11. Joseph, who married Nancy Skinner. (see family of Rhoda Skinner).

The family of James Spencer, Jr.
and his wife
Mary Abrams.

James Spencer, Jr. was born in England in 1730; served

in the Rev. War as follows:

Private in Capt. John Mann's Co. 1st Battalion

Phila. Co., Penna. Militia, (D.A.R. lineage pg.

365, Vol. 77).

Private Continental line (Penna. Archives Series

5, Vol. 4, pg. 198).

Commissioned Aug. 1777; ended Feb. 1782.

Copy of Land grant filed in Muskingum County, Ohio.

He owned land in Perry Co., Ohio, deed made in 1814.

In Oct. 1825, two months before his death he willed his land

to his youngest daughter, Sarah Wiswell and her son for his

"victualling and clothing". James Spencer, Jr. married Mary

Abrams. Their children were:

1. Rhoda, born Nov. 22, 1763; married Benjamin
        Jennings.

2. Thomas, born Oct. 26, 1765; married Margaret
        Armstrong.

3. Olive, born Oct. 28, 1767; married John McLean.

4. Jesse, born March 20, 1769; married Catherine
        _____.

5. William, born Feb. 3, 1772; married Martha Love.

6. Dinah, born March 10, 1774; married John McLean.

7. Elizabeth, born March 25, 1776; married Robert
        Skinner.

The family of James Spencer, Jr.
and his wife
Mary Abrams.

Continued.

8. Dorcas, born Nov. 10, 1778.

9. Benjamin, born Feb. 18, 1781; married
    Olive Kemp.

10. Drusilla, born Aug. 6, 1783; married William
    Forsythe.

11. James 3rd, born June 16, 1787; married Rachel
    Mitchell.

12. Sarah, born May 12, 1789; married John Wiswell.

The family of Elizabeth Spencer
and her husband
Robert Skinner.

Elizabeth Spencer, daughter of James Jr. and Mary (Abrams) Spencer, was born March 25, 1776; married Robert Skinner. The children of Robert and Elizabeth (Spencer) Skinner were:

1. Rebecca, married _____ Bartholomew.

2. Rhoda, married Jonathan Fickel.

3. Olive, married _____ McClure.

4. Eleanor, married _____ Yost.

5. William, married _____ Debolt.

6. Ruema, married _____ Yost.

7. John Skinner, married Rachel Johnson.
No children. Robert and
Elizabeth (Spencer) Skinner
are buried in the same Hop-
well Baptist Cemetery as James.

The family of Rhoda Skinner
and her husband
Jonathan Fickel

Rhoda Skinner, daughter of Robert and Elizabeth (Spencer) Skinner was born   ; married Jonathan Fickel March 26, 1817 in Fairfield County, Ohio, by William Tait; lived in Perry Co., Ohio until 1841 when they moved to Franklin Co., Ohio. The children of Jonathan and Rhoda (Skinner) Fickel were:

1. Rebecca, who married May 16, 1858 Lewis Latham.

2. Mary, who married _____ Armstrong.

3. Betty, who married Feb. 19, 1843 Aaron Skinner.

4. Sarah, who married Dec. 22, 1848 John Bowser.

5. Eliza, who married _____ Bailey.

6. Nelson, who married Apr. 7, 1859 Rachel Acton.

7. Alford, who married Oct. 4, 1849 Susannah Heise.

8. William.

9. Robert.

10. George, who married Dec. 21, 1849 Mary B. Tarr.

11. Joseph, born Feb. 15, 1836; married Nancy Skinner.
    Their child was:

    a. Isaac H. Fickel, who married Aug. 29, 1878 Clarissa V. Curry; divorced 1894. Their child was:
        Edith, born Jan. 7, 1880; married Quincy Leckrone Aug. 19, 1896.
        Their sons are:
            Walter Leckrone, born June 2, 1897; married Ethel Brown.
            Howard Leckrone, born Apr. 26, 1900; married Eleanor Wise, Jan. 3, 1927. Their children are:

The family of Rhoda Skinner
and her husband
Jonathan Fickel

Continued.

Walter Thomas Leckrone,
born March 23, 1930.

James Howard Leckrone,
born Feb. 5, 1936.

The family of Joseph G. Fickel*
and his wife
Nancy Tannehill.

Joseph G. Fickel, born Aug. 4, 1780; died Oct. 15, 1860;

married ca 1801 to Nancy Tannehill; born March 12, 1777,

died July 18, 1859.

Their children were:

1. Aletha, born June 7, 1802 married Edward
        Danison Dec. 18, 1823.

2. Jane, born Dec. 5, 1803 married Charles
        Gordon Dec. 5, 1822.

3. Jonathan, born Oct. 12, 1805 married Jane
        O'Hare April 12, 1827. Jonathan
        died Aug. 17, 1844.

4. Isaac, born Feb. 2, 1808 married first
        Catherine Eby Sept. 9, 1828. He
        married second, Elizabeth Jones
        Apr. 7, 1833.

5. Alexander, born July 25, 1810; died Aug. 17,
        1817.

6. Aaron, born Dec. 5, 1812; died Aug. 12, 1822.

7. William, born Sept. 9, 1815 married first
        Susannah Ward Nov. 2, 1838. Mar-
        ried second, Mary Ann Pullen April
        8, 1841.

8. James, born Jan. 18, 1818 married Malvina
        Woolard July 2, 1844.

9. Elizabeth, born Jan. 18, 1818; died Apr. 7,
        1819.

10. Mary Ann, born Feb. 25, 1820 died Sept. 25,
        1898; married Sept. 8, 1842 to
        Wm. Brown.

11. George, born Sept. 26, 1822 married Hannah
        Harding Apr. 18, 1846.

* Joseph G. Fickel was a grandson of Michael Fickel.
   Line untraced.

William Dusenberry
of
New Jersey and Ohio

William Dusenberry, was born near Bethlehem, in Sussex County, New Jersey, April 6, 1757, died at the village of Sego, in Madison Township, Perry County, Ohio, March 23, 1846. He was buried in his family burial ground on his farm at Sego.

Survivors File No. 8, 372, Revolutionary War Section of the Department of the Interior, Washington, D. C. gives his record as follows:

"William Dusenberry, born April 6, 1757; resided at Bethlehem, New Jersey when he enlisted in April 1776, (nearly three months before the Declaration of Independence was signed) and served under Col. Joseph Beaver, in monthly tours, as follows:

1776, three months, under Captains Carhart; Thomas Jones; William Farrow.

1777, four months, under Captains Francis Lock; John Stryker; Growendyke.

1778, four months, under Captains Cornopius Johnson; Lock; Growendyke; and Jones.

Winter 1778/9, six months under Captain Adam Hope.

1779, two weeks under same Captain.

He was in the engagements of Amboy, Farm Road, Second River, Short Hills, Hillstone and White Hills.

He always held the rank of Sergeant, but sometimes

served as Comissary and as Quartermaster.

He died in Perry County, Ohio, March 23, 1846."

On page 209 of the History of Perry County, published in 1883, is found the following:

Of the first settlers in Perry County were three men who came from Sussex County, New Jersey, about 1800; one of these was William Dusenberry, who settled at the junction of Jonathan's Creek and Turkey Run, and is traditionally known as the first settler in Madison Township. Mr. Dusenberry was a Revolutionary Soldier, and was 19 years of age when that war broke out, and remembered seeing George Washington. He lived up to the time of his death where, as above mentioned, he had located, and was the first man buried in the honors of war in the township. He was buried on his own farm.

It is probable that his two youngest children, Catherine and Abigail were born in this township, and if so, it is quite likely that Catherine was the first child born in the township.

The part of the original grant upon which the family buriel ground of William Dusenberry is located is now owned by Mr. and Mrs. John W. Shaw, of Fultonham, Ohio, and they have recently granted to Joseph W. and Will J. Dusenberry, of Columbus, two of the great-grandsons of William Dusenberry, a perpetual easement in the old burial ground. These brothers have just completed cleaning up the grounds, and straightening up the old grave stones, the inscriptions of which are still perfectly legible. They also erected a substantial wrought iron fence around the burial plot, and in the center they have placed a large granite monument inscribed with the history and war record of their ancestor.

The burial ground is reached by going to the village of Sego, on the Zanesville and Maysville Pike, Route 22, about midway between Somerset and Fultonham, and walking up a lane at the west end of the village to the summit of the hill.

Abstract of the will of William Dusenberry,

Revolutionary Soldier.

Filed in New Lexington, Perry County, Ohio.

Will Book "B", page 211.

To son, John Dusenberry	50 acres
To son, Benjamin Dusenberry	50 acres
To son-in-law John Hummel	50 acres
To daughter, Elizabeth Henderson	50 acres
To son-in-law, Benjamin Fickel	50 acres
To daughter, Catherine Wise	50 acres
To son-in-law, Jacob Hummel	50 acres
To son-in-law, Joseph Fickel	50 acres

To grandson, William Dusenberry, (son of Benjamin).

All of the personal property left etc. to be divided among
my heirs to wit:

> John Dusenberry
> Henry Dusenberry
> Benjamin Fickel
> Catherine Wise
> Jacob Hummel
> Jacob Fickel

Executors: John Dusenberry and friend William Moore dated
June 30, 1840.

Witnesses: John Hammer and Barnet Hammer.

In addition to the foregoing I will that my wife, Catherine be allowed to reside and enjoy the mansion house for
her natural life.

The family of William Dusenberry
and his first wife
Elizabeth _____.

William Dusenberry, married first, Elizabeth _____.
She was born April 28, 1761; died August 20, 1797. Their
children were:

1.   Henry, born Nov. 1, 1780; married July 31,
        1816 to Rachael Ashbrooke.

2.   Sarah, born Jan. 21, 1782; died Aug. 23, 1784.

3.   Mary, born Tuesday, June 3, 1783; married
        Aug. 1, 1805 to Joseph D. Fickel.

4.   John, born Wednesday, Aug. 4, 1784; married
        first to Christina Reed; married
        second to Phoebe Burkey March 12,
        1825. John Dusenberry died Aug.
        1, 1859.

5.   Rebecca, born Feb. 9, 1786; married Oct. 3,
        1805 to Benjamin Fickel.

6.   William, born Nov. 2, 1787.

7.   Benjamin, born Apr. 11, 1789; married Apr. 5,
        1821 to Charlotte Dennis.

8.   William, born Aug. 3, 1794.

9.   George, born June 11, 1795.

Note:
     The names of the children and dates of birth are
     from the Diary of William Dusenberry.

The family of John Dusenberry
and his first wife
Christina Reed.

John Dusenberry, son of William and Elizabeth (_____)
Dusenberry, born Aug. 4, 1784; died Aug. 1, 1859; married first, Christina Reed, Aug. 1, 1810. Their children
were:

1.   Jerusha, born 1815, died April 22, 1833;
            married William Rose.

2.   William, Removed to Iowa.

3.   John, Removed to Iowa.

4.   Thankful, born 1820; married George Rose.

The family of John Dusenberry
and his second wife
Phoebe Burkey. (Burley)

Continued.

1. Alford, born 1825; died 1894; married Apr. 28,
   1850 to Elizabeth Mitchell; born 1830;
   died 1912. A daughter Elizabeth McClain,
   born 1865, died 1936 is buried on the
   same lot.

2. Columbus, born May 13, 1839; died July 13, 1906;
   married July 15, 1860 in Perry Co., Ohio,
   to Sarah Jane Vanwey; born Apr. 18, 1838;
   died Feb. 4, 1926. Both buried in Ionia
   Cemetery, Ionia, Kan.
   Their children were:

   a. Adda Margaret, born Sept. 26, 1861;
      married Feb. 27, 1884 to Lewis Phillips.

   b. Albert Watson, born June 15, 1863; mar-
      ried Otelie Miller Aug. 1, 1894. Died
      Aug. 9, 1909; buried in Ionia Cemetery,
      Ionia, Kan.

   c. Alva Dayton, born Feb. 24, 1868; married
      Apr. 30, 1894 to Ella Kathryn Horrell.
      Their child is, Verneda Adda, born April
      27, 1900; married July 24, 1920 to Joe R.
      Beeler. They have two sons, namely:
        Joe R., Jr. born Aug. 13, 1924 at
        Beloit, Kansas. James Dayton, born
        Jan. 7, 1928 at Oakland Farm, Athens
        Township, Jewell Co., Kansas.

   d. Edith May, born May 27, 1870; married
      Aug. 19, 1891 to Winton Hoag; died Aug.
      8, 1921.

3. Henry.

4. Clarissa, born Feb. 1832; died July 14, 1870; married
   John Deaver.

5. Carolyn, died when about 18 years of age.

6. Elizabeth, died when about 25 years of age.

7. Perry, died unmarried.

8. Hannah, died Feb. 24, 1847 aged 12 years.

The family of Benjamin Dusenberry
and his wife
Charlotte Dennis

Benjamin Dusenberry, born April 11, 1789; was the son
of William and Elizabeth _____ Dusenberry. He married
in 1821, Charlotte Dennis. Their children were:

1. Henry, (deceased in 1865).

2. Aaron.

3. Elenor.

4. William.

5. Andrew Jackson, who married Sept. 21,
        1852, Sarah Hitchcock.

6. Adam.

7. Mary.

8. Joseph F.

9. John.

10. George.

11. Elizabeth.

12. Thomas.

13. Sarah Jane.

The family of Andrew Jackson Dusenberry
and his wife
Sarah Hitchcock

Andrew Jackson Dusenberry, son of Benjamin and Charlotte
(Dennis) Dusenberry, married Sarah Hitchcock Sept. 21,
1852. Their children were:

1. Joseph W., born June 22, 1858; died May
        7, 1936; married Ada McCarty,
        who was born Nov. 17, 1863;
        died Apr. 9, 1915. Joseph W.
        was a World War Veteran.

2. William J., born Jan. 16, 1865; died July 7,
        1935; never married; was World War
        Veteran.

3. Jemima, who married _____ Pletcher.

4. Jocie.

Dusenberry.

Buried in Green Lawn Cemetery, Columbus, Ohio:

Joseph W. Dusenberry, born June 22, 1858
            died May 7, 1936.
      American Red Cross World War service
            in France; Captain.

Will J. Dusenberry, born Jan. 16, 1865,
            died July 7, 1935.
      American Red Cross World War service
            in France; Captain.

Ada McCarty, wife of Joseph W. Dusenberry,
            born Nov. 17, 1863,
            died Apr. 9, 1915.

Abstract of the Will of John Dusenberry, Sr.,
of Hunterdon County, New Jersey.

Office of the Adj. General in Trenton.
Liber of Wills, 32, Folio 4.

    To wife, Johanna.

    To eldest sons, John and William.

    To Joshua Updyke, (son-in-law) and Mary,
        his wife.

    To three youngest sons, Sylvanus, Daniel,
        George.

        Wit:
            Samuel Eveland.
            John Garrison.
            George Garrison.

Sworn at Trenton the 28th day of May 1789 before me.

_____ Throckmorton.

Abstract of the Will of John Dusenberry, filed
in Morgantown, West Virginia.

Book 1, Page 33.

To son Henry.

To wife Sarah.

To son Samuel.

To daughter Sarah Clark.

To son Daniel.

To son Cornelius.

To daughter Lidia Cunningham and her
        children.

To daughter Mary.

To Katherine Wade and her children.

Signed Aug. 29, 1827

Wit:
    William Courtney.
    Michael Courtney.
    John Courtney.

John Dusenberry's wife was Sarah Carhart, daughter of
Major Cornelius Carhart. (See Carhart Genealogy, Page 62).

Abstract of the Will of Henry Dusenberry,
filed in Morgentown, W. Va.

Book 1, Page 239.

    To son George.

    To daughter Hester.

    To Liddy and Billy.

    To son John.

    To son Henry.

    To wife Rebecca.

    To daughter Sarah.

    To grandson Steenrod.

        Signed March 4, 1852.
        Son John, Executor.

Henry Dusenberry's wife was Rebecca Chambers.

Abstract of the Will of Jemima Dusenberry
of Taylorstown, Greene County, Penna.

Waynesburg, Penna.
Book 5, Page 333.

To Joan Smith.

To James B. Dusenberry.

To Jack Dusenberry.

To Thomas Benton Dusenberry.

To Lydia Donley.

To Josiah and Charles Dusenberry.

To Samuel Dusenberry.

Signed Dec. 28, 1874.

Wit:
   David Keener.
   Levi Fortney.

Abstract of the Will of Catherine Wise
of Boling Green Township,
Licking County, Ohio.

New Lexington, Perry County, Ohio.
Book 4, page 6.

        To Elizabeth Catherine Hummel.

        To William Hummel.

        To John Hummel.

        To Mary Jane Hummel (all of the ones mentioned,
                were children of William and Mary
                Hummel of Perry Co., Ohio).

        Land to be divided situated in Madison Township,
                Perry Co., conveyed to me by my
                father, Wm. Dusenberry, (deceased)
                by deed June 13, 1840.

                        Signed June 4, 1874.

                        Wit:
                            John Forsythe.
                            Alexander Melick.

Marriage Records

Dusenberry _____ Fickel

Filed in Zanesville, Muskingum County, Ohio.

Oct. 3, 1805,   Benjamin Fickel to Rebecca Dusenberry
                 By William Newell.

Oct. 1, 1805,   Joseph Fickle to Mary Dusenberry
                 By William Newell.

Aug. 15, 1815,   Lavina Dusenberry to James Johnston
                 By Isaac Brown J. P.

Oct. 22, 1816,   Rachel Fickle to Thomas Vansky (Vanscoy)
                 By Jacob Crooks J. P.

June 6, 1816,   Benjamin Dusenberry to Pressy Plummer
                 By Andrew Cusic, J. P.

Apr. 7, 1825,   Benjamin Fickle to Phebe Harris
                 By James Fleming

Aug. 1, 1815,   Daniel Fickle to Hetty Tipton (or Lipton)
                 By William Moore, J. P.

July 31, 1816,   Henry Dusenberry to Rachel Ashbrook
                 By James Culbertson

Aug. 5, 1810,   John Dusenberry to Christena Reed
                 By William Wilson J. P.

Marriage Records filed in Lancaster, Fairfield County, Ohio.

Aug. 12, 1812,   Sarah Fickle to George Crossan
                 By William Spencer J.P.

Nov. 28, 1816,   Isaac Fickle to Mary Fate (Tate).

Mar. 26, 1817,   Jonathan Fickle to Rhoda Skinner
                 By William Tait

Marriage Records

Dusenberry _____ Fickel

Filed in New Lexington, Perry County, Ohio.

Dec. 5, 1822,   Jane Fickle to Charles Gordon
                     By Wm. Williams J. P.

Dec. 18, 1823,   Elethia Fickle to Edward Danison
                     By Andrew Henkle J. P.

Apr. 12, 1827,   Jonathan Fickle to Jane O'Hare
                     By William Spencer J. P.

Oct. 30, 1827,   Joseph Fickle to Elizabeth Gatman
                     By Thomas Portor, J. P.

Jan. 22, 1830,   John Fickle to Rachel Barnet
                     By Alexander McCracken

July 23, 1825,   William Fickle to Sarah Zartman
                     By John Younkins

Mar. 14, 1833,   Nancy Fickle to James Hastel
                     By Benjamin Waddle M. G.

Oct. 29, 1835,   Mary Fickle to Jacob Bowman

Aug. 23, 1836,   Elizabeth Fickle to John Keller,
                     By Charles Fulton

Nov. 19, 1836,   Catherine Fickle to Abraham Bowser
                     By Samuel Curran J. P.

Nov. 3, 1836,   Rebecca Fickle to Wesley Davis
                     By Samuel Curran J. P.

Mar. 2, 1837,   Mary Ann Fickle to William R. House
                     By George Reed J. P.

Nov. 2, 1838,   William Fickle to Susannah Ward
                     By Henry Fernandis M. G.

Feb. 14, 1839,   Rachel Fickle to Levi Schisler
                     By Samuel Curran

Sept. 9, 1828,   Isaac Fickle to Catherine Eby.
                     By C. Henkle.

Apr. 17, 1834,   Henry Fickel to Dolly Robey
                     By Samuel Curran J. P.

Continued

Aug. 30, 1820,   Sarah Dusenberry to John Hummel

Apr. 5, 1821,   Benjamin Dusenberry to Charlotte Dennis

Sept. 4, 1821,   Sarah Dusenberry to William Hall (Hull)
                  By John W. Patterson M. G.

Mar. 12, 1825,   John Dusenberry to Phebe Burkey (or *Burley*)

Oct. 30, 1838,   William Dusenberry to Elizabeth Winder

Apr. 28, 1850,   Alfred Dusenberry to Elizabeth Mitchell

Sept. 21, 1852,   Andrew J. Dusenberry to Sarah Hitchcock

May 10, 1827,   Abagail Dusenberry to Jacob Hummel
                  By George Deboth V.D. M.

Apr. 23, 1828,   Catherine Dusenberry to William Wise
                  By H. M. Davis

Feb. 24, 1825,   Jenna Dusenberry to John A. Cramer
                  By Thomas Moore V. D. M.

Sept. 5, 1841,   Jacob Fickel to Catherine Craig
                  By George Reed J. P.

June 27, 1840,   James Fickle to Amanda Woolard

Dec. 17, 1840,   Nancy Fickle to George Robey

Mar. 18, 1841,   Harriett Fickle to Henry Taylor

Sept. 8, 1842,   Mary Ann Fickle to William Brown

Oct. 7, 1843,   Sarah Fickle to Jacob Youker (Youkins)

Mar. 16, 1844,   Mariah Fickle to Ruel Skinner

Apr. 18, 1846,   George Fickel to Hannah Harding

Nov. 18, 1852,   Bartholomew Fickle to Martha Dennis
                  By James Shreaves J. P.

Aug. 29, 1878,   Isaac Fickle to Clara V. Curry
                  By Elder Barker

Oct.   1838,   Sarah Fickle to George Latta.

The family of Selathial Hamilton, M. D.
and his wife
Sarah J. Watson.

Selathial Hamilton, son of John and Julia (Scott)

Hamilton was born Nov. 5, 1825 in Monongalia Co., W. Va.

He married Sarah J. Watson. He attended school in Zanes-

ville, Ohio. Later went to Indiana where he studied

medicine with Dr. Luther Hess, a relative. He was a

pioneer physician of Roseburg, Oregon where he died,

aged about 86.

Their children were:

1.   Walter S., a physician of Roseburg,
          Oregon.

2.   James Watson, (Judge) an attorney of
          Roseburg, Oregon.

3.   J. F., an attorney of Astoria, Oregon.

4.   Inez, wife of Frank J. Micelli, an at-
          torney of Roseburg, Oregon.

5.   Charles L., an attorney of Roseburg,
          Oregon.

6.   Julia, wife of W. C. Washburn, of Junction
          City, Oregon.

7.   Luther Hess, a physician of Portland,
          Oregon.

8.   Estelle, wife of _____ Richardson, of
          Roseburg, Oregon.

The family of James McCord
and his wife
Martha Burch.

James McCord married Martha Burch in Ohio County,

W. Va., March 24, 1791. (By James Hughes). Record

in Wheeling, W. Va.   Their children were:

1.   William, born 1792, died 1868; married
          Dorcas _____. Buried near
          Cynthiana, Pike Co., Ohio,
          died 1868.

2.   Benjamin, born ca 1800.

3.   Enoch D., born March 5, 1802 near Marietta,
          Ohio; died July 28, 1880 in Pike
          County, Ohio; married first, Polly
          (Mary) Elliott. She died ca 1829,
          leaving twins, Nimrod Elliott Mc-
          Cord and Mariah McCord, who married
          _____ Dewey.

      Enoch married second, Sarah Blair.

4.   John.

5.   James, Jr., was a physician, moved to California.

There were probably other children, names unknown.

The family of Nimrod Elliott McCord
and his wife
Sarah Bridwell.

Nimrod Elliott McCord, son of Enoch D. and Polly (Elliott) McCord was born Feb. 26, 1827 died Dec. 19, 1906 in Bainbridge, Ohio.   He married Sarah Bridwell, who was born May 14, 1832; died June 7, 1901.   Buried in Bainbridge. Their children were:

1.   Joseph Wesley McCord, who married Laura
        Jane Kelley.

2.   Mary, who married William Sprinkle.

3.   Belle, who married Homer Huling Sept.
        17, 1885. Had a daughter
        Charlene, who married Earl
        Stewart.

4.   Ella, never married.

5.   Frank, married Mary _____.

The family of Joseph Wesley McCord
and his wife
Laura Jane Kelley

Joseph Wesley McCord, son of Nimrod Elliott and Sarah (Bridwell) McCord was born in Bainbridge, Ohio, Sept. 11, 1850; died in Columbus, Ohio, April 27, 1927; married Sept. 17, 1872 in Bainbridge, Laura Jane Kelley; born Dec. 20, 1853, died Oct. 13, 1905. She was the daughter of Rev. Asbury Clarke and Caroline (Hamilton) Kelley.

Their children were:

1. Caroline Kelley McCord, born July 24, 1873.
2. Myrtle Estelle, born June 22, 1875.
3. Etta Hoyt McCord, born Sept. 20, 1877.
4. Josephine Clarke, born Aug. 27, 1879.

Joseph Wesley McCord and his wife Laura Jane Kelley are buried in Green Lawn Cemetery, Columbus, Ohio.

Joseph Wesley McCord married second, Mabel Helen Root. There were no children by this marriage.

The family of Caroline Kelley McCord
and her husband
Walter Scott Butterfield

Caroline Kelley McCord, daughter of Joseph Wesley
and Laura Jane (Kelley) McCord, was born in Bainbridge, Ohio, July 24, 1873; married Walter Scott
Butterfield of Battle Creek, Michigan.
Their children were:

1. Caroline Hamilton Butterfield, married
         Clarence B. Allen of Grand
         Rapids, Michigan. Their chil-
         dren are:
              Caroline, Barbara and
              James Scott.

2. Laura McCord Butterfield, married Jesse
         Page.   Their children are:
              Laura, Jesse Jr., and
              Michael Kelley.

3. Julia Scott Butterfield, married George
         Herman Jr. They live in Auburn
         N. Y. and have one son.

4. Helen Butterfield, married Paul Berry.
         They live in Pasadena, Calif.
         have two children.

Caroline McCord divorced from Walter Butterfield.

Married second, Jack Vandervoort Hurd. No children

by this marriage.

The family of Myrtle Estelle McCord
and her husband
Nathan Woodward

Myrtle Estelle McCord, daughter of Joseph Wesley

and Laura Jane (Kelley) McCord was born in Bain-

bridge, Ohio, June 22, 1875; married Nathan Woodward

who was born May 13, 1873 at St. Williams, Ontario.

Their children are:

1.   Elizabeth, born Oct. 30, 1898; married
            Thomas Bradfield Meek. Their
            children are:
                  Mary Elizabeth, born July 14,
                  1924 and Thomas Bradfield, Jr.,
                  born Oct. 9, 1925.

                  Elizabeth Woodward Meek, divor-
                  ced from Thomas Meek.

2.   Robert McCord Woodward, born Apr. 20, 1910;
            married Flora Powell. Their children
            are twin girls, born Jan. 2, 1939,
            named:
                  Vera Rankin Woodward.
                  Virginia Powell Woodward.

The family of Etta Hoyt DeLong
and her husband
Paul Augustus DeLong

Etta Hoyt McCord, daughter of Joseph Wesley and Laura Jane (Kelley) McCord was born Sept. 20, 1877 at Rees Station, Ohio; married Paul Augustus DeLong of Columbus, Ohio. Their children:

1. Laura Jane, born Oct. 1, 1901; married
         Nov. 30, 1924, John Roney of
         Middletown, Ohio.
         Their children are:
              John Jr. (Jack)
              Catherine.

2. Paul Jr., died April 27, 1940; unmarried.

The family of Josephine Clarke McCord
and her husband
Fred Vercoe.

Josephine Clarke McCord, daughter of Joseph Wesley
and Laura Jane (Kelley) McCord was born in Columbus,
Ohio, Aug. 27, 1879; married Sept. 11, 1899 to Fred
Vercoe, who was born June 24, 1876 in Columbus. His
parents, George and Mary Vercoe came to this country
from Cornwall County, England.

Their children are:

1.   Joseph McCord, born July 9, 1900; married
            Oct. 8, 1925 to Adrienne Lunette
            Smith; born July 27, 1901. Their
            children are:
                Joanne Thrall, born Dec. 26,
                1926.
                Fred 3rd, born Oct. 15, 1928.

2.   Fred, Jr., born June 12, 1902; married Aug.
            14, 1929 to Olga Erickson; born
            Jan. 30, 1907. Their child is:
                Mary Jo, born July 26, 1930.

3.   Richard Caslow, born March 27, 1907; married
            Aug. 12, 1933 to Pauline Lybarger;
            born June 15, 1905 in Gambier, Ohio.

Adrienne L. (Smith) Vercoe, daughter of Marshall and
Cora (Smith) Smith.   See National numbers 101471 and
203103.

Olga (Erickson) Vercoe, daughter of Carl and Dorothy Hay
(Hai) Erickson.

Pauline (Lybargar) Vercoe, daughter of Paul and Eva Lybargar.
See Lybarger Genealogy.

The family of Sanford B. Scott
and his wife
Hannah Tibbs

Sanford B. Scott, son of Col. James Scott and his
wife Amelia (Daugherty) Scott, was born 1812; died
1868. He received the Col. James Scott homeplace;
married Hannah Tibbs. They settled near Anderson,
Indiana. Their children were:

1. James, never married.

2. Bushrod T., died in Anderson, Ind.

3. Louisa, married Samuel Frum. Their
        children were:

   a. Francis Scott Frum; mar-
      ried Charles Dent, the
      son of Dr. George Dent
      and his second wife, Thelma
      Triplett.

   b. _____, who married John
      Trevillian.

   c. Elizabeth; married Fred Hough.

   This family lived in Morgantown.

4. William, M. D., lived in Anderson, Indiana.

5. Fanny.

6. Jennie, married _____ Davis.

7. John, (a druggist) died in Kansas.

8. Isabelle, married Schraken Gast, of Anderson,
        Indiana.
        Their children were:

   a. Mildred, married Earl Roseberry.

   b. Caroline, resides with her father.

9. Mary, married George Vanse of Morgantown, W. Va.

The family of Bushrod W. Scott
and his second wife
Lucy Chapman

Bushrod W. Scott, son of Col. James Scott and his wife
Amelia (Daugherty) Scott, was born September 1808; married first, Henrietta Clark; married second Lucy Chapman,
who died March 1870. Bushrod Scott died Aug. 3, 1871 at
Sulpher Springs, Ind.   Their children were:

1.   James, died in infancy.

2.   Sanford, died in infancy.

3.   Elmira, died in infancy.

4.   Althia Ann, died aged 4 years.

5.   Oliver Perry, born 1844; died 1862 in the
            Army; buried in National Cemetery,
            Nashville, Tenn.

6.   Caroline, born 1846; died 1909, married
            _____ Ringo. Jane Ringo, her
            daughter married John Menefee,
            son of Alexander Smith Menefee.

7.   Florence, died aged six months.

8.   William T., born 1848; married Kate
            Hollinger.

9.   George, born 1854; died aged 29 years.

10.   Walter M., married Addie Osborn.

11.   Emma Amelia, born 1859; living in 1938;
            married Rufus Mann, who died
            in 1917 aged 79 years. They
            lived at Sulpher Springs, Ind.

The family of William T. Scott
and his wife
Juliet Marchand.

William T. Scott, son of Col. James Scott and his
wife Amelia (Daugherty) Scott, was born Nov. 5,
1795; died March 18, 1862; married Juliet Marchand
of Uniontown, Pa., who died Sept. 28, 1889.
William T. Scott and his wife left Virginia May 29,
1831 and came to Indiana, they lived in the vicinity
of Alexandria, Ind. The children of William T. Scott
and his wife Juliet Marchand were:

1. Eliza Ann, married Amos Collins.

2. Daniel T., married Jemima Brooks (Banks)

3. Isabelle, married Dr. John Horne, a
        Scotsman. She died in 1895.

4. James P., married Lucia Clark.

5. Amelia, married William Crim. Their
        children were:

        a. Harriett, married Chas. Daniels.
        b. Juliet, married Dale Critten-
            berger.
        c. William.

        All lived in Anderson, Indiana.

6. Jane, never married.

7. Rawley, married _____ Veach; lived in Henry
        Co., Indiana.

8. Antoinette, married Dr. Joseph Pugh.

9. Caroline, married Robert Hanna.

The family of David Scott
and his wife
Marjory Harrison

David Scott, son of Col. James and Amelia (Daugherty) Scott, was born in 1791; died 1875, aged 85 years and 8 months; married Marjory Harrison, daughter of Richard Harrison, Jr. (who was a nephew of Benjamin Harrison) and his wife Nancy Martin, daughter of Col. Charles and Elizabeth (Burrows) Martin. David Scott and Marjory Harrison were married April 9, 1819. Marjory Harrison Scott died in 1870, aged about 71 years. Both buried in Granville Cemetery, Morgantown, W. Va. Their children were:

1. Matilda, born Jan. 7, 18___, married Morgan Boggess.

2. Harriett, born Aug. 16, 1822; married Charles G. Martin.

3. Caroline Sidonia, born Oct. 15, 1834; died March 3, 1838.

4. Virginia, born Sept. 11, 1839; married Dr. Marmaduke Dent. Their son William married Elizabeth Jane Evans, their daughter Jessie M. Dent married Carl P. Lash.

5. Caroline Louise, born Feb. 13, 1826; married Sanford G. W. Morrison. Their children were:

   a. Frank (M. D.) married May Copenhaver.
   b. Chas. (Atty.) married Agnes J. _____.
   c. Mary Adaline, married Charles Dille.
   d. Florence S., married James Watson.
   e. Virginia, married Abraham Lash.
      Their son Carl married Jessie

The family of David Scott
and his wife
Marjory Harrison

Continued

6. Ann Amelia, born June 29, 1831; married
        Sept. 1853, Charles Brown.
        Their children were:

        a. Myrtle, married _____
            Courtney of Maidsville,
            W. Va.

        b. Florence, married E. E.
            Davis; lives near Denver.

The Dent Family

Thomas Dent, born 1630/31. Served in the Indian Wars;
came from Gisborough, England; died 1676 in Maryland;
High Sheriff of St. Mary's County, Md. in 1664; one
of the Justices of the above mentioned county; a del-
egate from said county in 1669; married Rebecca Wil-
liamson (Wilkinson), daughter of Rev. William Wilk-
insin. Their sons:

Major Wm. B. Dent, born ca 1652; died 1704; State Atty.
for St. Mary's, Calvert and Charles Counties, Md.;
married Feb. 8, 1684, to Elizabeth Fowke (b. ca 1664).
daughter of Col. Gerrard Fowke (d. 1669) and his wife,
Ann Chandler (a widow). Their son:

Peter Dent, born 1693; Bap. 1/13/1694; died 1757; will
probated 11/23/1757; married Mary Brooke, daughter of
Thomas Brooke of Prince George County, Md. Their son
Walter B. Dent, born 1725; died 1760; wife's name un-
known. The widow married to Mr. Hampton. Their son:
John Dent, born May 1755; died Sept. 20, 1840; Lt. in 9th
Va. Reg.; first sheriff of Monongalia County, W. Va.;
member of Virginia Assembly; Justice of Peace; married
Margaret Evans (born 1763; died Nov. 23, 1851), daughter
of Col. John Evans, first clerk of Monongalia Co., W. Va.
Ref: Colonial Families of the U. S. Vol. 3, pages 152-155
by McKenzie.

Also see: Vol. 3 of Compendium of American Genealogies,
Page 533.

The family of Captain John Dent
and his wife
Margaret Evans

Elizabeth, who married Rawley Martin.

George, who died in New Orleans.

Dudley, who married Mahala Berkshire.

Nancy Ann, who married Felix Scott.

Nimrod, who married Susan Graham.

Peggy, who married John Rochester.

Enoch, who married Julia Gapen.

James, who married Dorcas Berkshire.

Marmaduke, who married Sarah Price.

Ann Arah, who married Peter Fogle.

Rawley, who married Marie Miller.

John Evans, born Jan. 26, 1783, married Rebecca
              Hamilton.

John Evans Dent, son of Capt. John Dent, and his wife
Margaret (Evans) Dent was born Jan. 26, 1783 at the
Caption John Dent homestead in Grant District, Monongalia County, W. Va., near the unincorporated village
of Laurel Point, on Dents Run. He married Rebecca
Hamilton (b. Jan. 23, 1786; died Aug. 13, 1832.) on
March 18, 1804 in Monongalia Co., W. Va. She was the
daughter of William Hamilton and his wife Susannah
Brown. (Note: William Hamilton's will on file in Muskingum County, Ohio). See a following page for abstract
of same.

The family of Captain John Dent

Continued

He married second, Mary Cowen Irwin (born Apr. 26, 1802;

died Feb. 28, 1887) in Putnam Co., Ill. He died at Magnolia,

Ill. March 18, 1868.

The children of John Evans Dent and his wife Rebecca (Hamilton)

Dent were:

1. Gillie Evans, born 1805 in Monongalia Co., W. Va.
   Married William Cowen who was born in
   1798 in Maryland, died in Magnolia, Ill.
   They were married in 1824 near Zanesville,
   Ohio.

2. Rebecca.

3. Zilpha, born in Muskingum Co., Ohio, March 17, 1811;
   married in 1832 to Elisha Swan in Putnam
   County, Ill.; she died July 19, 1894.

4. George.

5. Margaret, born July 18, 1814; married Livingston
   Roberts; died Jan. 28, 1892 in Putnam
   County, Ill.

6. Susan, married _____ Myers. She was born July 5,
   1820.

The child of John Evans Dent and Mary Cowen Irwin was:

7. Orlando, born June 29, 1840; married Rachel
   Hart. He died March 28, 1883.

Marmaduke Dent, son of Capt. John Dent and his wife Margaret

(Evans) Dent, was born Feb. 25, 1801; studied medicine under

Dr. Enos Daugherty of Morgantown. In 1927 he married Sarah
Price, daughter of Col. William Price of
Kingwood.

Note: For complete record of this family
see Wiley's Hist. Monongalia County.

Abstract of the Will of William Hamilton
filed in
Zanesville, Muskingum County, Ohio

Dated Feb. 1813.

Mentions wife Susannah.

Mentions son Benjamin of Monongalia Co., W. Va.

Mentions son William.

Mentions son Samuel.

Mentions daughters:

Cassandra Harrison.

Rachel Smith (deceased).

Elizabeth Manley.

Rebecca Dent.

Susannah Hiatt.

Mentions grandchildren:

The sons and daughters of his daughter, Rachel
Smith (deceased):
William John and Darius Smith,
Cassandra and Susannah Smith.

Requests that his wife keep Mary Chadwick and the black girl,

Jane.

Executors:

William and Samuel Hamilton.

Requests that my son Benjamin attend to my business in Monongalia County and that William and Samuel
attend to all other part. To see that
this my last Will and Testament be executed.

Wit:
Thomas Nesbit
George Dils
E. B. Morgan

Marriage records of the Hamilton Family
of
Monongalia Co., W. Va.
and of
Muskingum Co., Ohio

William Hamilton to Hannah Ewings, Oct. 18, 1810.
            By Robert Manley.

Susannah Hamilton to William Heath (Hiatt), Oct. 12,
            1810.

Cassandra Hamilton to Joseph Harrison, Feb. 6, 1797.

      (Children of William and Susannah Hamilton)

Cassandra Smith to John German, Nov. 7, 1816, by D. Young.

      (Grandchild of William and Susannah Hamilton)

Note:

      William Hamilton was born in 1760 near Baltimore,
      Maryland. There he married Susannah Brown.
      Moved to Laurel Point, (near Morgantown, W. Va.)
      in 1789. On their way, a son later Rev. William
      Hamilton, was born May 1, 1789 in Penn. In about
      1800 he went with his parents to Ohio, locating
      in Hopewell Township, Muskingum County. This
      family later moved to Marysville, Union County,
      Ohio.
      See Hist. of Union Co., for sketch of family.

      This William Hamilton did not serve in the Revol-
      utionary War, nor did he serve in the War of 1812.
      He appears to have been a nephew of John Hamilton,
      born 1730; the first of the Hamilton family to
      settle in Monongalia Co., Va.

The family of Felix Scott

Felix Scott, son of Capt. David and Judith (Cunningham)
Scott, was born Dec. 13, 1785; married Nancy (Ann) Dent,
in 1807, who was born at the Dent homestead, Monongalia
County, W. Va., May 23, 1789. She was the daughter of
Captain John Dent and his wife Margaret (Evans) Dent.
Margaret (Evans) Dent was the daughter of Col. John Evans,
a Revolutionary Soldier. The children of Felix and Ann
(Dent) Scott were:

1. Lindian, born Aug. 23, 1809; died Dec. 16, 1846.
2. Lucinda, born Aug. 23, 1809; died Sept. 7, 1862.
3. Haswell, born May 11, 1811;
4. George, born Mar. 22, 1813; died Feb. 17, 1885.
5. Presley, born Dec. 25, 1814; died Apr. 25, 1867.
6. Harmacintha, born Sept. 16, 1816; died Feb. 21, 1860.
7. A daughter, born Nov. 13, 1819, died Nov. 13, 1819.

On April 5, 1821, Felix Scott married second, Ellen Castlio of
St. Charles County, Missouri, his first wife having died in
above mentioned county Nov. 23, 1819.

The children of Felix Scott and his second wife, Ellen Castlio
Scott were:

8.   Nancy, born June 12, 1823; died Mar. 7, 1867.
9.   Ellen, born Nov. 28, 1824; died June 28, 1890.
10. Harriett, born Feb. 10, 1826; died Jan. 9, 1846.
11. A daughter, born Feb. 10, 1826; died Feb. 26, 1846.
12. Juliet, born Mar. 15, 1827; died
13. Felix, born July 2, 1829; died Nov. 9, 1879.
14. Marion, born Mar. 11, 1831; died May 4, 1881.
15. Marchand, born Sept. 23, 1832; died Sept. 26, 1835.
16. Bushrod, born Aug. 28, 1834; died Nov. 3, 1842.
17. Mariah, born Aug. 31, 1836; died Aug. 13, 1844.
18. Nimrod, born Aug. 14, 1838; died Spt. 27, 1862.
19. Harrison, born Feb. 6, 1840; died
20. Rodney, born Jan. 29, 1842; died Mar. 10, 1910.

The family of Felix Scott

Continued

21.   Melissa, born May 19, 1844; died Dec. 24, 1844.
22.   Jane Linn, born Sept. 21, 1846; died Nov. 7, 1861.

Felix Scott was killed by the Indians in Nevada near

Winnemucca in the fall of 1858.

The family of Lindian Scott
and her husband
Jonathan Comegys

Lindian Scott, was born Aug. 23, 1809, daughter of Felix

and Nancy Ann (Dent) Scott, was married Feb. 23, 1827 to

Jonathan Comegys in St. Charles Co., Mo.   Jonathan Comegys

was born _____ 1800, was the son of Abraham Comegys, a native

of Maryland, who moved to West Virginia, and shortly after

in 1817, to St. Charles Co., Mo.

Lindian Scott Comegys died Dec. 16, 1846 in St. Charles County,

Mo., Jonathan Comegys died in Polk County, Oregon, Dec. 31, 1852.

Their children were:

1.   Cynthia Ann, born June 28, 1828; died July 10, 1854;
        married Samuel A. Spencer. She died on
        Beaver River in Utah while en route to
        Oregon with her husband and child, Lindian.
        The daughter Lindian married _____ Hostetter
        and went to live in San Jose, California.

2.   Coleman E., born Feb. 18, 1830; died Sept. 29, 1834.

3.   Hannah, born Nov. 1, 1832; died Nov. 1832.

4.   William, born Nov. 22, 1833; died April 8, 1896; mar-
        ried Nov. 16, 1864 to Lovina Ann Ball.
        Their children were:
        a.   Ida, born Nov. 25, 1867; married
        July 29, 1891 to Edmond J. Doneen.
        They had one child, Harold Comegys
        Doneen born Mar. 28, 1896. Harold
        C. Doneen married Oct. 16, 1921 to
        Hortense Francis Harrild, daughter
        of Fred and Eva Van Fleet Harrild
        and reside at Farmington, Wash.

The family of Lindian Scott
and her husband
Jonathan Comegys

Continued

        b.   Felix, born Aug. 15, 1869, resid-
ing with his mother at Amith, Ore.

5.   Nancy, born Aug. 26, 1836; died Jan. 5, 1889. Married Dec. 6, 1860 to Samuel Baxter. He
died Oct. 5, _____.   Their children were:
    a.   Delia, born July 1, 1873; married
Sept. 11, 1900 to Willard Converse,
reside in Palo Alto, Calif. Their
children were:
        Willard Baxter Converse, born Mar.
27, 1906; and Victoria Ellen, born
Aug. 9, 1908.

6.   George, born Dec. 16, 1838; died Feb. 7, 1904; married
in 1863 to Elain (Evaline) Stewart.
Their children were:
    a.   Harriett, born June 18, 1864; married
S. Joseph Daniels of Seattle, Wash.
Their children were:
        Bessie, born Sept. 1, 1890; Emery
Clair, born Feb. 14, 1892.
Lucile Mildred, born Jan. 27, 1895.
Carrie Elinor, born Aug. 29, 1897.
    b.   A child who died in infancy.

George Comegys married second Margaret A. Bell on May
28, 1873; the children of this marriage:

    c.   Ralph, born Apr. 24, 1874.
    d.   Horace, born Oct. 5, 1876.
    e.   Calude, born Mar. 9, 1882.

All reside in Farmington, Washington.

The family of Lindian Scott
and her husband
Jonathan Comegys

Continued

       d.   Horace, married Maggie L. Blackmore.
           Their children were:
              Thadus, born Oct. 13, 1906.
              Ansel, born _____, died _____.

       e.   Claude, born Mar. 9, 1882; married
           Dec. 25, 1912 to A n Marie Arters
           of Mill Village, Penna. Their child-
           ren were:
              George (Robert George), born Dec.
              17, 1913.
              Margaret Frances, born Dec. 5, 1915.
              Jean Idele, born Sept. 9, 1919.

7.   William H. Harrison, born Jan. 1840; _____.

8.   Presley, born Aug. 8, 1842; died July 18, 1862.

9.   Henry C., born Nov. 15, 1844; died Nov. 9, 1921;
        married May 7, 1878 to Sarah Lysons. (married
        at Kalama, Washington).
        Their children were:

       a.   Roy W., born May 5, 1880; married
           Sept. 23, 1908 to Katharine Simonton.

       b.   Eva, born Apr. 23, 1883; married
           _____ Payne.

       c.   Elsie, born Jan. 24, 1864.

       Sarah Lysons Comegys, died at Snohomish,
       Washington May 4, 1926.

The family of Lucinda Scott
and her husband
Benjamin Comegys

Lucinda Scott, born Aug. 23, 1809, daughter of Felix Scott

and Ann (Dent) Scott, was married in St. Charles County,

Missouri, March 25, 1828, to Benjamin Comegys.   He died

in Missouri July 9, 1844; she died in Lane County, Oregon,

Sept. 7, 1862. Their children were:

1.   Wilmer, born _____ 1823; died _____ 1883. He died
        unmarried in Harney Co., Oregon; is buried
        in Eugene Oregon.

2.   Presley, born July 2, 1830; died Dec. 7, 1917; mar-
        ried Jan. 15, 1863 to Melzina Duncan of
        Lane Co., Oregon. Their children were:

        a.   Viloa, born July 7, 1864; married
                Dec. 18, 1884 to W. W. Withers. He
                died Feb. 7, _____.   Their child,
                Frank Withers was born June 7, 1886.

        b.   Nellie, born Apr. 30, 1866; married
                Oct. 31, 1892 to O. A. Campbell.
                Their children were Kenneth and Coyle.

                Nellie Campbell resides at the Lexington
                Apt's, Seattle, Wash. Both her sons are
                reported to be married.

        Melzina Comegys, wife of Presley Comegys, died April
                20, 1866.

        He married second, July 21, 1872, Melinda J. Clearwater.
                They had one child:

        c.   Arthur, born Sept. 30, 1873; died Aug.
                31, 1906.

3.   Nimrod, died in Harney Co., Oregon. Married Nov. 3, 1864
        to Sarilda Ann Duncan.

The family of Lucinda Scott
and her husband
Benjamin Comegys

Continued

She died in Burns, Oregon March 19, 1917.
Their children were:

a. Charles W., lived at Diamond, Oregon;
married July 2, 1895 in Harney Co.,
Oregon to Nora May Marshall.
Their children were:
Lloyd, about 22 years in 1926.
Elmer, married in Aug. 1926 to
_____ Anderson.
Opal, married Sept. 1925 to Oscar
Courtright of Smith River, Calif.

b. Lucinda, married Gus Schroeder, they
had one son, Eston, who perished in
the Silver Lake fire.

c. Anna, married Feb. 22, 1896 to Charles
Hains, who died May 1916 in Portland,
Oregon. Their children were:
Hazel, born Apr. 1897; married Apr.
21, 1921 to Dr. Dorman Leonard of
Portland, Oregon. Their children
were:
Anna Jean, born Oct. 23, 1923.
Another child born in 1926.
Wilber, born Apr. 23, 1900;
married Sept. 21, 1920 to Mary
Jenkins. They reside at Diamond,
Oregon. Their children were:
John,
Charles
Marie, who was born Aug. 13, 1907.

d. Fay, of Narrows, Oregon. Was married Dec.
28, 1897 to Ollie McKenzie. Their children
were:
Mohler, who married Edna Hines. They
had one daughter.
Lafe, who married in 1925 to
Dorothy _____.

e. Sydney, of Diamond, Oregon, married July 7,
1899 to Anna Anderson and had August, age
about 18 years in 1926 and Georgia, age about
6 years in 1926.

The family of Hazwell Scott
and his wife

Hazwell Scott, son of Felix and Ann Dent Scott, was born May 11, 1811. He left home in early youth and was supposed to have gone to Texas. After the War between the States a rumor came to his relatives in Oregon that he had served as a high officer in the Confederate Army. Nothing is known to the family of his history after leaving home.

The family of George Scott
and his wife
Harriett R. Phillips

George Scott, son of Felix and Nancy Ann (Dent) Scott,

was born March 22, 1813; married Nov. 19, 1838 to

Harriett R. Phillips. She died April 2, 1909. The

children of George and Harriett (Phillips) Scott were:

1. Jennie, who married Louis L. Luddington. Their
   children were Harriett, who married _____
   Dryburg and Louis, who died at the age of
   7 years.

2. Thomas Felix, born Nov. 29, 1841; died May 31, 1915;
   married Dec. 2, 1874 to Laura Alice McCann.
   She died June 27, 1893. He died May 31,
   1915. Their children were:
   a. Jennie, who married H. H. Owen and
      have two sons and three daughters.
      Two sons died in the World War.
   b. Harry F., married Mary Henson; have
      three sons and two daughters.
   c. Mabel.
   d. Harriett, married Andrew Miller; have
      one son.
   e. Alonza, married Maggie Osborn, have
      two sons and one daughter.
   f. Laura.
   g. Florence, married Edmond Jordon,
      have five sons and one daughter.
   h. An unnamed son.

3. Henry Scott, born 1846; died 1908; married to Edith
   Ellen McCann. Their children were:
   a. George Scott, born 1870, died 1885.
   b. Georgia, married Robert Overstreet
      and have two children, Marjorie and
      Robert.
      Lived at Nyssa, Oregon.
   c. Tennie.

The family of George Scott
and his wife
Harriett Phillips

Continued

d. Mattie.
e. Editha Ellen, married and lives in
Siox City, Iowa. Her mother lives
with her.
f. Ellen Edith (twin of above), lives
in Kansas City, Mo.
g. Emma.

4. George Z., who married Jennie Russel. She resides
at 1239 West 49th Street, Los Angeles,
Calif. Their children were:
Pearl and Louis, both said
to have married.

George Scott, son of Felix Scott went to California overland
when gold was discovered there and after six months returned
by water. In 1870 he settled in Ford Co., Ill. His son,
Thomas Felix Scott enlisted in the Union Army in 1862, Company
B, 86th, Ill. Inf.; was mustered into service at Peoria Aug.
27th. The first important engagement in which he participated
was at Perryville, Ky. He went with Sherman on the celebrated,
from Atlanta to the sea. In a skirmish at Kenesaw Mountain
he was wounded in the left arm by a Minie ball and was granted
a furlough and returned home. Subsequently, he was transferred
to Company K, 155th. Ill. Inv. and was promoted to rank of
first Lieutenant. He participated in many engagements and
when the war was over was honorably discharged in 1865. The
sword he carried is in his oldest son's possession.

The family of Presley Scott
and his first wife
Jane Cottle

Presley Scott, son of Felix and Nancy Ann (Dent) Scott,

was born Dec. 25, 1814; died April 25, 1885 at or near

Helena, Montana.   He married _____ Jane Cottle, and

to them was born one child:

>   Bushrod, who died in 1862, unmarried,
>   at Boise, Idaho.

The family of Presley Scott
and his second wife
Elizabeth Shelton

Presley Scott, married second April 15, 1851 Elizabeth

Shelton.   She died at Eugene, Oregon Nov. 2, 1890.

Their children were:

1.   Rawleigh, born Dec. 4, 1851; died Jan. 2, 1920;
            married in Oct. 1874 to Nellie Cooley.
            He died Jan. 2, 1920,. Mrs. Scott died
            May 31, 1924 at Smith River, California.

2.   Robert Scott, born Feb. 5, 1853; married July 4,
            1878 to Martha Lindley. He married
            second Oct. 28, 1882 to Clara Crook.
            She died ca 1886.
            He married third on Jan. 31, 1898 to
            Mrs. Anna C. Quaques and to them was born
               Hazel Asella on Feb. 16, 189 , and
               Robert Jr., on March 24, 1902.

3.   Jennie, born Feb. 17, 1854; married Dec. 5, 1882
            John Tryon and had the following children:

            a. Ethel, born Sept. 13, 1883; mar-
               ried Mar. 25, 1902 David Goodlow
            and had two sons,
               John Goodlow, born Dec. 25,
               1902, and
               Lloyd Goodlow, born Sept. 16,
            1912.

The family of Presley Scott
and his second wife
Elizabeth Shelton

Continued

    c. Hilda, born Mar. 11, 1888; married
        Mar. 23, 1916 to Charles Gribling
        and had one son,
            Charles Tryon Gribling, born
            March 12, 1819.
            Hilda Tryon Gribling died May
            30, 1919.
    d. Presley, born Aug. 3, 1890; married
        _____; had one son, Marlin Tryon,
        born Sept. 11, 1916.
    e. Fay, born Jan. 10, 1893; married
        Sept. 5, 1915 to Will Crone, had
        one daughter
            Margaretta Crone, born Sept. 30,
            1916.
    f. George, born Feb. 12, 1895; married
        Feb. 14, 1918 to Theresa Hussey; had
        one son
            Murray, born Jan. 4, 1920.

4. Presley, married in 1887 to Melissa Caroline Boggs,
        born Dec. 12, 1856. He died Nov. 24, 1909;
        she died Feb. 25, 1905.
        Their children were:
    a. Loraine, born Dec. 30, 1890; married
        Dec. 11, 1913 to James Patterson Smart,
        now reside at Salem, Oregon. They had
            Margaret Loraine, born July 10, 1915
            and James Scott, born Aug. 4, 1919.

5. James, married in 1881 to Linda Rollins. Their children

        were:
    a. Maude, born 1882; married _____ Bazell of
        Holbrook, Arizona. Had one child
            Wilma, born ca 1910.
    b. May, born 1886; married Wm. Chadwick, Jr.
        born ca 1912.
    c. James Eugene, born 1889; died 1899.

James Scott, Sr., married second Marguerite
Purcell in 1911.

The family of Presley Scott
and his second wife
Elizabeth Shelton

Continued

6. Lucy, married Feb. 10, 1884 to William Matthews;
        died Feb. 2, 1892. Their children were:

            a. J. Frank, born Oct. 22, 1886; died
                _____; married Dec. 10, 1910 to
                Kate Beiler.
                They reside at Long Beach, Calif.

            b. Walter Scott, born Oct. 28, 1888;
                died Feb. 2, 1890.

        Lucy (Scott) Matthews married second on
        Apr. 19, 1894 to Wm. Scarborough; he
        died Oct. 23, 1924.

        Lucy (Scott) Matthews Scarborough, married
        third Nov. 19, 1925 to Welby J. Edwards,
        now residing at Mayville, Oregon.

7. George, married June 8, 1898 to Adah M. Stroup.
        Their children were:

            a. George Jr., born Aug. 31, 1899.

            b. Marion Elizabeth, born May 23, 1903;
                married Oct. 2, 1926 to Ellsworth
                Reynolds Menhennet at Mesa Arizona.

            c. John Francis, born April 4, 1905.

Notes of Interest

Robert Scott, son of Presley Scott, organized the bank
at Salt River Valley at Mesa, Arizona in 1906 and was
its president up to 1924, when his failing health caused
him to resign. He served as a member of the Arizona
Legislature.

James Scott, son of Presley Scott, was a member of the
Territorial Legislature of Arizona and also of the Con-
stitutional Convention which framed the constitution
of the State when it was admitted to the Union. He
served later as State Senator from Nevaja County.

George Scott, Jr. graduated from the University of Arizona
in 1925 as an electrical engineer.

George Comegys and Henry Comegys were successful lawyers
and then took up the banking business, which both followed
to the end of their lives and in which they have been successful and were succeeded by their sons.

Eva Comegys, daughter of Henry Comegys after graduating
from the University of Washington, took three years post
graduate work at Columbia University, N. Y., and one year
in Europe; has been an instructor in the Oregon Agricultural
College for several years past.

Raleigh Scott, son of Presley Scott, served in the Legislature of the State of Oregon.

The family of Hermacintha Scott
and her husband
Obediah Keithly

Hermacintha Scott, born in Monongalia County, W. Va.;

Sept. 16, 1816; married April 28, 1836 in St. Charles

County, Mo., to Obediah Keithly; born Jan. 24, 1814.

She died April 21, 1860 in Vernon County, Mo., her

husband died July 22, 1906 in Caroll Co., Mo. Their

children were:

1. Marchand, born June 7, 1837; died Apr. 25, 1898;
    married Hannah Elizabeth Brothers and
    had
        Marion Obediah, born Mar. 10, 1861;
        died Dec. 11, 1904,
        Mattie, born Oct. 31, 1863
        Marchand Bee, born Apr. 5, 1865.

2. Neri, born July 15, 1839; died Apr. 12, 1911.

3. Felix Scott, born Dec. 2, 1841; died Apr. 9, 1917.

4. George W., born Feb. 7, 1844; died July 14, 1900.

5. Calvin Harrison, born Mar. 21, 1846; died Sept.
    23, 1876.

6. Ann Elizabeth, born Feb. 19, 1849; died July 30,
    1920.

7. Mary Ellen, born Aug. 15, 1851; died May 16, 1883.

8. Marion Obediah, born Feb. 19, 1854; died July 10,
    1859.

9. Hermacintha, born Sept. 18, 1856.

10. Marion Dudley, born Jan. 22, 1860; died Feb. 11,
    1861.

The Marchand Family

Dr. David Marchand (1719/1761) was a descendant of the Huguenots who fled to Switzerland upon the revocation of the Edict of Nantes.

He was a physician and practiced in the town of Sonvilier, Canton of Berne, Switzerland. He came to America in 1754 in the vessel "Nancy", landing at Philadelphia, Penna.

He married in 1744 to Judith Marie (Jacot) Gentle (died 1789). She was a physician also and practiced medicine with her husband in Hagerstown, Maryland.

Their son Dr. David Marchand, Jr., (1746/1809) settled at Sewickley, Penna. He married in 1766 Elizabeth Kaemerer (1744/1817). Dr. David Marchand, Jr., was a Surgeon and Captain in the 3rd Company of the 2nd Penna. line of Westmoreland County, Penna., in the Revolutionary War.

The children of Dr. David Marchand, Jr., and his wife Elizabeth (Kaemerer) Marchand were:

1. Catherine, born Mar. 8, 1767; married Wm. Shron.

2. Elizabeth, born Nov. 5, 1768; married John Kuhns.

3. Susannah, born Oct. 13, 1770; married Adam Rodebaugh.

4. Dr. Daniel, born Dec. 8, 1773; married Betsy Scott.

5. Judith, born Nov. 12, 1772; married in 1787 Henry Lutzenheiser.

6. Esther, born Aug. 23, 1779; married Christian Brenneman.

Continued

7.   Dr. David Jr., born Dec. 10, 1776; of
        Westmoreland, Penna.

8.   Dr. Louis, born June 23, 1782; died Jan.
        11, 1857; married in 1823 to
        Susannah Sackett, daughter of
        Dr. Samuel Sackett of Connecticut,
        who was a surgeon in the Rev. War.
        Susannah (Sackett) Marchand died
        Nov. 8, 1870, aged 73, years and
        left six children.

Ref: Compendium of American Genealogy,
        Vol. 4, Page 221.

        Wills and deeds in Uniontown, Pa.

        Cyclopedia of Fayette County, Pa.
        by Wiley, Page 554.

The family of Betsy Scott
and her husband
Dr. Daniel Marchand

Betsy Scott, born 1773; died 1822, was the daughter of
Captain David and Judith (Cunningham) Scott, married ca
1799 to Dr. Daniel Marchand of Uniontown, Pa.   Their
children were:

1.   Juliet, who married March 21, 1826 to Wm.
        Tingle Scott; born Sept. 5, 1801,
        in N. Liberty, Va., died in Ander-
        son, Indiana Sept. 26, 1889. They
        had ten children.

2.   Ann (Nancy), born Sept. 1802; died Apr. 4, 1878;
        unmarried.

3.   Dr. Benj. Rush, born 1804; died Jan. 1864; known
        as "The Good Physician", married Ann
        Fullerton, daughter of William and
        Jane Irwin Fullerton. Their children
        were:

        a.   Elizabeth Jane, born 1832; died
             1850.
        b.   John, born 1842; died 1867 in
             Philadelphia, Pa.

4.   Norval David, born 1806; died 1849 en route to
        California, married first to Matilda
        Goodwin, second to Jane Goodwin, White-
        head, a widow with one son, Laurence.
        Both were daughters of Aaron and Mar-
        garet McCullough Goodwin.

5.   Elizabeth Jane, born March 1810; died 1834; mar-
        ried first to Dr. William Morris, of
        Fayette Co., Pa. (died 1828), married
        second to David Oldham. Her children
        were:

        a.   Springer Morris.
        b.   Matilda Oldham.
        c.   William Oldham.

The family of William Dusenberry
and his second wife
Catherine Compton.

10. Elizabeth, born Feb. 8, 1799; married Jan. 1,
        1816 to Robert Henderson.

11. Sarah, born July 3, 1801; married Aug. 31, 1820
        to John Hummel.

12. Catherine, born Apr. 17, 1804; married Mar. 20,
        1828 to William Wise.

13. Abigail, born Oct. 23, 1806; married May 10,
        1827 to Jacob Hummel.

Soldiers of the American Revolution
contained in this
Genealogy.

Jonathan Arnold.

Benjamin Chesney.

John Combs (Coombs).

Elisha Clayton.

Ensign William Cunningham.

Captain John Dent.

Captain James Daugherty.

Sergeant William Dusenberry.

Colonel John Evans.

Lieutenant Benjamin Fickel.

Daniel Fickel.

Isaac Fickel.

Stephen Gapen.

Captain John Hamilton.

Dr. David Marchand.

Charles Martin.

Colonel Zackweil Morgan.

Jacob Pindall.

Captain Phillip Pindall.

Thomas Pindall.

Alexander Scott.

Benjamin Scott.

Captain David Scott.

Jacob Scott.

James Scott (of Richwood).

James Spencer.

William Wilson.

War of 1812.

Captain Forbes Britton.

Aaron Barker.

John Chipps.

Henry Dusenberry.

Colonel Dudley Evans.

Captain Joseph Neeley.

Major James Pindall.

Edward Pindall.

Noah Ridgeway.

Lieut. Colonel James Scott.

Major David Scott.

Rawley Scott.

Sergeant John Shively.

Lieutenant Michael Shively.

Caleb Trippet.

Richard Tibbs.

Major Thomas P. Moore.

The family of Lindian Scott
and her husband
Jonathan Comegys

Lindian Scott, was born Aug. 23, 1809, daughter of Felix
and Nancy Ann (Dent) Scott, was married Feb. 23, 1827 to
Jonathan Comegys in St. Charles Co., Mo. Jonathan Comegys
was born _____ 1800, was the son of Abraham Comegys, a native
of Maryland, who moved to West Virginia, and shortly after
in 1817, to St. Charles Co., Mo.
Lindian Scott Comegys died Dec. 16, 1846 in St. Charles County,
Mo., Jonathan Comegys died in Polk County, Oregon, Dec. 31, 1852.
Their children were:

1. Cynthia Ann, born June 28, 1828; died July 10, 1854;
        married Samuel A. Spencer. She died on
        Beaver River in Utah while en route to
        Oregon with her husband and child, Lindian.
        The daughter Lindian married _____ Hostetter
        and went to live in San Jose, California.

2. Coleman E., born Feb. 18, 1830; died Sept. 29, 1834.

3. Hannah, born Nov. 1, 1832; died Nov. 1832.

4. William, born Nov. 22, 1833; died April 8, 1896; mar-
        ried Nov. 15, 1864 to Lovina Ann Ball.
        Their children were:
    a. Ida, born Nov. 25, 1867; married
        July 29, 1891 to Edmond J. Doneen.
        They had one child, Harold Comegys
        Doneen born Mar. 28, 1896. Harold
        C. Doneen married Oct. 16, 1921 to
        Hortense Francis Harrild, daughter
        of Fred and Eva Van Fleet Harrild
        and reside at Farmington, Wash.

The family of Lindian Scott
and her husband
Jonathan Comegys

Continued

b. Felix, born Aug. 15, 1869, resid-
    ing with his mother at Amith, Ore.

5. Nancy, born Aug. 26, 1836; died Jan. 5, 1889. Mar-
    ried Dec. 6, 1860 to Samuel Baxter. He
    died Oct. 5, _____.   Their children were:
    a. Delia, born July 1, 1873; married
        Sept. 11, 1900 to Willard Converse,
        reside in Palo Alto, Calif. Their
        children were:
            Willard Baxter Converse, born Mar.
            27, 1906; and Victoria Ellen, born
            Aug. 9, 1908.

6. George, born Dec. 16, 1838; died Feb. 7, 1904; married
    in 1863 to Elain (Evaline) Stewart.
    Their children were:
    a. Harriett, born June 18, 1864; married
        S. Joseph Daniels of Seattle, Wash.
        Their children were:
            Bessie, born Sept. 1, 1890; Emery
            Clair, born Feb. 14, 1892.
            Lucile Mildred, born Jan. 27, 1895.
            Carrie Elinor, born Aug. 29, 1897.
    b. A child who died in infancy.

George Comegys married second Margaret A. Ball on May
    28, 1873; the children of this marriage:

    c. Ralph, born Apr. 24, 1874.
    d. Horace, born Oct. 5, 1876.
    e. Calude, born Mar. 9, 1882.

All reside in Farmington, Washington.

The family of Lindian Scott
and her husband
Jonathan Comegys

Continued

    d.   Horace, married Maggie L. Blackmore.
        Their children were:
           Thadus, born Oct. 13, 1906.
           Ansel, born _____, died _____.

    e.   Claude, born Mar. 9, 1882; married
        Dec. 25, 1912 to A n Marie Arters
        of Mill Village, Penna. Their child-
        ren were:
           George (Robert George), born Dec.
           17, 1913.
           Margaret Frances, born Dec. 5, 1915.
           Jean Idele, born Sept. 9, 1919.

7.   William H. Harrison, born Jan. 1840; _____.

8.   Presley, born Aug. 8, 1842; died July 18, 1862.

9.   Henry C., born Nov. 15, 1844; died Nov. 9, 1921;
        married May 7, 1878 to Sarah Lysons. (married
        at Kalama, Washington).
        Their children were:

    a.   Roy W., born May 8, 1880; married
        Sept. 23, 1908 to Katharine Simonton.

    b.   Eva, born Apr. 23, 1883; married
        _____ Payne.

    c.   Elsie, born Jan. 24, 1864.

    Sarah Lysons Comegys, died at Snohomish,
    Washington May 4, 1926.

The family of Lucinda Scott
and her husband
Benjamin Comegys

Lucinda Scott, born Aug. 23, 1809, daughter of Felix Scott

and Ann (Dent) Scott, was married in St. Charles County,

Missouri, March 25, 1828, to Benjamin Comegys. He died

in Missouri July 9, 1844; she died in Lane County, Oregon,

Sept. 7, 1862. Their children were:

1. Wilmer, born _____ 1823; died _____ 1883. He died
    unmarried in Harney Co., Oregon; is buried
    in Eugene Oregon.

2. Presley, born July 2, 1830; died Dec. 7, 1317; mar-
    ried Jan. 15, 1863 to Melzina Duncan of
    Lane Co., Oregon. Their children were:

    a. Vilos, born July 7, 1864; married
        Dec. 18, 1884 to W. W. Withers. He
        died Feb. 7, _____. Their child,
        Frank Withers was born June 7, 1886.

    b. Nellie, born Apr. 30, 1866; married
        Oct. 31, 1892 to O. A. Campbell.
        Their children were Kenneth and Coyle.

        Nellie Campbell resides at the Lexington
        Apt's, Seattle, Wash. Both her sons are
        reported to be married.

    Melzina Comegys, wife of Presley Comegys, died April
        20, 1866.

    He married second, July 21, 1872, Melinda J. Clearwater.
        They had one child:

    c. Arthur, born Sept. 30, 1873; died Aug.
        31, 1906.

3. Nimrod, died in Harney Co., Oregon. Married Nov. 3, 1864
    to Sarilda Ann Duncan.

The family of Lucinda Scott
and her husband
Benjamin Comegys

Continued

She died in Burns, Oregon March 19, 1917.
Their children were:

a. Charles W., lived at Diamond, Oregon;
    married July 2, 1895 in Harney Co.,
    Oregon to Nora May Marshall.
    Their children were:
        Lloyd, about 22 years in 1926.
        Elmer, married in Aug. 1926 to
        _____ Anderson.
        Opal, married Sept. 1925 to Oscar
        Courtright of Smith River, Calif.

b. Lucinda, married Gus Schroeder, they
    had one son, Eston, who perished in
    the Silver Lake fire.

c. Anna, married Feb. 22, 1896 to Charles
    Hains, who died May 1916 in Portland,
    Oregon. Their children were:
        Hazel, born Apr. 1897; married Apr.
        21, 1921 to Dr. Dorman Leonard of
        Portland, Oregon. Their children
        were:
            Anna Jean, born Oct. 23, 1923.
            Another child born in 1926.
            Wilber, born Apr. 23, 1900;
            married Sept. 21, 1920 to Mary
        Jenkins. They reside at Diamond,
        Oregon. Their children were:
            John,
            Charles
        Marie, who was born Aug. 13, 1907.

d. Fay, of Narrows, Oregon. Was married Dec.
    28, 1897 to Ollie McKenzie. Their children
    were:
        Mohler, who married Edna Hines. They
        had one daughter.
            Lafe, who married in 1925 to
            Dorothy _____.

e. Sydney, of Diamond, Oregon, married July 7,
    1899 to Anna Anderson and had August, age
    about 18 years in 1926 and Georgia, age about
    6 years in 1926.

The family of Hazwell Scott
and his wife

Hazwell Scott, son of Felix and Ann Dent Scott, was born May 11, 1811. He left home in early youth and was supposed to have gone to Texas. After the War between the States a rumor came to his relatives in Oregon that he had served as a high officer in the Confederate Army. Nothing is known to the family of his history after leaving home.

The family of George Scott
and his wife
Harriett R. Phillips

George Scott, son of Felix and Nancy Ann (Dent) Scott,

was born March 22, 1813; married Nov. 19, 1838 to

Harriett R. Phillips. She died April 2, 1909. The

children of George and Harriett (Phillips) Scott were:

1. Jennie, who married Louis L. Luddington. Their
    children were Harriett, who married _____
    Dryburg and Louis, who died at the age of
    7 years.

2. Thomas Felix, born Nov. 29, 1841; died May 31, 1915;
    married Dec. 2, 1874 to Laura Alice McCann.
    She died June 27, 1893. He died May 31,
    1915. Their children were:
    a. Jennie, who married H. H. Owen and
        have two sons and three daughters.
        Two sons died in the World War.
    b. Harry F., married Mary Henson; have
        three sons and two daughters.
    c. Mabel.
    d. Harriett, married Andrew Miller; have
        one son.
    e. Alonza, married Maggie Osborn, have
        two sons and one daughter.
    f. Laura.
    g. Florence, married Edmond Jordon,
        have five sons and one daughter.
    h. An unnamed son.

3. Henry Scott, born 1846; died 1908; married to Edith
    Ellen McCann. Their children were:
    a. George Scott, born 1870, died 1885.
    b. Georgia, married Robert Overstreet
        and have two children, Marjorie and
        Robert.
        Lived at Nysse, Oregon.
    c. Tennie.

The family of George Scott
and his wife
Harriett Phillips

Continued

        d.   Mattie.
        e.   Editha Ellen, married and lives in
               Siox City, Iowa. Her mother lives
               with her.
        f.   Ellen Edith (twin of above), lives
               in Kansas City, Mo.
        g.   Emma.

4.   George Z., who married Jennie Russel. She resides
        at 1239 West 49th Street, Los Angeles,
        Calif. Their children were:
               Pearl and Louis, both said
               to have married.

George Scott, son of Felix Scott went to California overland
when gold was discovered there and after six months returned
by water. In 1870 he settled in Ford Co., Ill. His son,
Thomas Felix Scott enlisted in the Union Army in 1862, Company
B, 86th, Ill. Inf.; was mustered into service at Peoria Aug.
27th. The first important engagement in which he participated
was at Perryville, Ky. He went with Sherman on the celebrated,
from Atlanta to the sea. In a skirmish at Kenesaw Mountain
he was wounded in the left arm by a Minie ball and was granted
a furlough and returned home. Subsequently, he was transferred
to Company K, 155th. Ill. Inv. and was promoted to rank of
first Lieutenant. He participated in many engagements and
when the war was over was honorably discharged in 1865. The
sword he carried is in his oldest son's possession.

The family of Presley Scott
and his first wife
Jane Cottle

Presley Scott, son of Felix and Nancy Ann (Dent) Scott,
was born Dec. 25, 1814; died April 25, 1885 at or near
Helena, Montana. He married _____ Jane Cottle, and
to them was born one child:

> Bushrod, who died in 1862, unmarried,
> at Boise, Idaho.

The family of Presley Scott
and his second wife
Elizabeth Shelton

Presley Scott, married second April 15, 1851 Elizabeth
Shelton. She died at Eugene, Oregon Nov. 2, 1890.
Their children were:

1. Rawleigh, born Dec. 4, 1851; died Jan. 2, 1920;
   married in Oct. 1874 to Nellie Cooley.
   He died Jan. 2, 1920,.. Mrs. Scott died
   May 31, 1924 at Smith River, California.

2. Robert Scott, born Feb. 5, 1853; married July 4,
   1878 to Martha Lindley. He married
   second Oct. 28, 1882 to Clara Crook.
   She died ca 1886.
   He married third on Jan. 31, 1898 to
   Mrs. Anna C. Quaques and to them was born
   Hazel Azella on Feb. 16, 189 , and
   Robert Jr., on March 24, 1902.

3. Jennie, born Feb. 17, 1854; married Dec. 5, 1882
   John Tryon and had the following children:

   > a. Ethel, born Sept. 13, 1883; mar-
   > ried Mar. 25, 1902 David Goodlow
   > and had two sons,
   >   John Goodlow, born Dec. 25,
   >   1902, and
   >   Lloyd Goodlow, born Sept. 16,
   >   1912.

The family of Presley Scott
and his second wife
Elizabeth Shelton

Continued

      c.   Hilda, born Mar. 11, 1888; married
         Mar. 23, 1916 to Charles Gribling
         and had one son,
             Charles Tryon Gribling, born
             Merch 12, 1819.
             Hilda Tryon Gribling died May
             30, 1919.
      d.   Presley, born Aug. 3, 1890; married
         _____; had one son, Marlin Tryon,
         born Sept. 11, 1916.
      e.   Fay, born Jan. 10, 1893; married
         Sept. 5, 1915 to Will Crone, had
         one daughter
             Margaretta Crone, born Sept. 30,
             1916.
      f.   George, born Feb. 12, 1895; married
         Feb. 14, 1918 to Theresa Hussey; had
         one son
             Murray, born Jan. 4, 1920.

4.   Presley, married in 1887 to Melissa Caroline Boggs,
         born Dec. 12, 1856. He died Nov. 24, 1909;
         she died Feb. 25, 1905.
         Their children were:
      a.   Loraine, born Dec. 30, 1890; married
         Dec. 11, 1913 to James Patterson Smart,
         now reside at Salem, Oregon. They had
             Margaret Loraine, born July 10, 1915
             and James Scott, born Aug. 4, 1919.

5.   James, married in 1881 to Linda Rollins. Their children

      were:
      a.   Maude, born 1882; married _____ Bazell of
         Holbrook, Arizona. Had one child
             Wilma, born ca 1910.
      b.   May, born 1886; married Wm. Chadwick, Jr.
         born ca 1912.
      c.   James Eugene, born 1889; died 1899.

      James Scott, Sr., married second Marguerite
      Purcell in 1911.

The family of Presley Scott
and his second wife
Elizabeth Shelton

Continued

6. Lucy, married Feb. 10, 1884 to William Matthews;
        died Feb. 2, 1892. Their children were:

        a. J. Frank, born Oct. 22, 1886; died
            _____; married Dec. 10, 1910 to
            Kate Beiler.
            They reside at Long Beach, Calif.

        b. Walter Scott, born Oct. 28, 1888;
            died Feb. 2, 1890.

        Lucy (Scott) Matthews married second on
        Apr. 19, 1894 to Wm. Scarborough; he
        died Oct. 23, 1924.

        Lucy (Scott) Matthews Scarborough, married
        third Nov. 19, 1925 to Welby J. Edwards,
        now residing at Mayville, Oregon.

7. George, married June 8, 1898 to Adah M. Stroup.
        Their children were:

        a. George Jr., born Aug. 31, 1899.

        b. Marion Elizabeth, born May 23, 1903;
            married Oct. 2, 1926 to Ellsworth
            Reynolds Menhennet at Mesa Arizona.

        c. John Francis, born April 4, 1905.

Notes of Interest

Robert Scott, son of Presley Scott, organized the bank
at Salt River Valley at Mesa, Arizona in 1906 and was
its president up to 1924, when his failing health caused
him to resign.   He served as a member of the Arizona
Legislature.

James Scott, son of Presley Scott, was a member of the
Territorial Legislature of Arizona and also of the Con-
stitutional Convention which framed the constitution
of the State when it was admitted to the Union. He
served later as State Senator from Nevaja County.

George Scott, Jr. graduated from the University of Arizona
in 1925 as an electrical engineer.

George Comegys and Henry Comegys were successful lawyers
and then took up the banking business, which both followed
to the end of their lives and in which they have been successful and were succeeded by their sons.

Eva Comegys, daughter of Henry Comegys after graduating
from the University of Washington, took three years post
graduate work at Columbia University, N. Y., and one year
in Europe; has been an instructor in the Oregon Agricultural
College for several years past.

Raleigh Scott, son of Presley Scott, served in the Legislature of the State of Oregon.

The family of Hermacintha Scott
and her husband
Obediah Keithly

Hermacintha Scott, born in Monongalia County, W. Va.;
Sept. 16, 1816; married April 28, 1836 in St. Charles
County, Mo., to Obediah Keithly; born Jan. 24, 1814.
She died April 21, 1860 in Vernon County, Mo., her
husband died July 22, 1906 in Caroll Co., Mo. Their
children were:

1. Marchand, born June 7, 1837; died Apr. 25, 1898;
   married Hannah Elizabeth Brothers and
   had
      Marion Obediah, born Mar. 10, 1861;
      died Dec. 11, 1904,
      Mattie, born Oct. 31, 1863
      Marchand Bee, born Apr. 5, 1865.

2. Neri, born July 15, 1839; died Apr. 12, 1911.

3. Felix Scott, born Dec. 2, 1841; died Apr. 9, 1917.

4. George W., born Feb. 7, 1844; died July 14, 1900.

5. Calvin Harrison, born Mar. 21, 1846; died Sept.
   23, 1876.

6. Ann Elizabeth, born Feb. 19, 1849; died July 30,
   1920.

7. Mary Ellen, born Aug. 15, 1851; died May 16, 1883.

8. Marion Obediah, born Feb. 19, 1854; died July 10,
   1859.

9. Hermacintha, born Sept. 18, 1856.

10. Marion Dudley, born Jan. 22, 1860; died Feb. 11,
    1861.

The Marchand Family

Dr. David Marchand (1719/1761) was a descendant of the
Huguenots who fled to Switzerland upon the revocation of
the Edict of Nantes.

He was a physician and practiced in the town of Sonvilier,
Canton of Berne, Switzerland. He came to America in 1754
in the vessel "Nancy", landing at Philadelphia, Penna.

He married in 1744 to Judith Marie (Jacot) Gentle (died
1789). She was a physician also and practiced medicine
with her husband in Hagerstown, Maryland.

Their son Dr. David Marchand, Jr., (1746/1809) settled at
Sewickley, Penna. He married in 1766 Elizabeth Kaemerer
(1744/1817). Dr. David Marchand, Jr., was a Surgeon and
Captain in the 3rd Company of the 2nd Penna. line of
Westmoreland County, Penna., in the Revolutionary War.

The children of Dr. David Marchand, Jr., and his wife
Elizabeth (Kaemerer) Marchand were:

1. Catherine, born Mar. 8, 1767; married Wm. Shron.

2. Elizabeth, born Nov. 5, 1768; married John Kuhns.

3. Susannah, born Oct. 13, 1770; married Adam Rodebaugh.

4. Dr. Daniel, born Dec. 8, 1773; married Betsy Scott.

5. Judith, born Nov. 12, 1772; married in 1787 Henry
   Lutzenheiser.

6. Esther, born Aug. 23, 1779; married Christian
   Brenneman.

The Marchand Family

Continued

    7.   Dr. David Jr., born Dec. 10, 1776; of
                Westmoreland, Penna.

    8.   Dr. Louis, born June 23, 1782; died Jan.
                11, 1857; married in 1823 to
                Susannah Sackett, daughter of
                Dr. Samuel Sackett of Connecticut,
                who was a surgeon in the Rev. War.
                Susannah (Sackett) Marchand died
                Nov. 8, 1870, aged 73, years and
                left six children.

Ref: Compendium of American Genealogy,
         Vol. 4, Page 221.

         Wills and deeds in Uniontown, Pa.

         Cyclopedia of Fayette County, Pa.
         by Wiley, Page 554.

                        The family of Betsy Scott
                             and her husband
                          Dr. Daniel Marchand

Betsy Scott, born 1773; died 1822, was the daughter of

Captain David and Judith (Cunningham) Scott, married ca

1799 to Dr. Daniel Marchand of Uniontown, Pa.   Their

children were:

    1.   Juliet, who married March 21, 1826 to Wm.
               Tingle Scott; born Sept. 5, 1801,
               in N. Liberty, Va., died in Ander-
               son, Indiana Sept. 26, 1889. They
               had ten children.

    2.   Ann (Nancy), born Sept. 1802; died Apr. 4, 1878;
               unmarried.

    3.   Dr. Benj. Rush, born 1804; died Jan. 1864; known
               as "The Good Physician", married Ann
               Fullerton, daughter of William and
               Jane Irwin Fullerton. Their children
               were:

               a. Elizabeth Jane, born 1832; died
                   1850.
               b. John, born 1842; died 1867 in
                   Philadelphia, Pa.

    4.   Norval David, born 1806; died 1849 en route to
               California, married first to Matilda
               Goodwin, second to Jane Goodwin, White-
               head, a widow with one son, Laurence.
               Both were daughters of Aaron and Mar-
               garet McCullough Goodwin.

    5.   Elizabeth Jane, born March 1810; died 1834; mar-
               ried first to Dr. William Morris, of
               Fayette Co., Pa. (died 1828), married
               second to David Oldham. Her children
               were:

               a. Springer Morris.
               b. Matilda Oldham.
               c. William Oldham.

The family of William Dusenberry
and his second wife
Catherine Compton.

10. Elizabeth, born Feb. 8, 1799; married Jan. 1,
    1816 to Robert Henderson.

11. Sarah, born July 3, 1801; married Aug. 31, 1820
    to John Hummel.

12. Catherine, born Apr. 17, 1804; married Mar. 20,
    1828 to William Wise.

13. Abigail, born Oct. 23, 1806; married May 10,
    1827 to Jacob Hummel.

Soldiers of the American Revolution
contained in this
Genealogy.

Jonathan Arnold.

Benjamin Chesney.

John Combs (Coombs).

Elisha Clayton.

Ensign William Cunningham.

Captain John Dent.

Captain James Daugherty.

Sergeant William Dusenberry.

Colonel John Evans.

Lieutenant Benjamin Fickel.

Daniel Fickel.

Isaac Fickel.

Stephen Gapen.

Captain John Hamilton.

Dr. David Marchand.

Charles Martin.

Colonel Zackwell Morgan.

Jacob Pindall.

Captain Phillip Pindall.

Thomas Pindall.

Alexander Scott.

Benjamin Scott.

Captain David Scott.

Jacob Scott.

James Scott (of Richwood).

James Spencer.

William Wilson.

War of 1812.

Captain Forbes Britton.

Aaron Barker.

John Chipps.

Henry Dusenberry.

Colonel Dudley Evans.

Captain Joseph Neeley.

Major James Pindall.

Edward Pindall.

Noah Ridgeway.

Lieut. Colonel James Scott.

Major David Scott.

Rawley Scott.

Sergeant John Shively.

Lieutenant Michael Shively.

Caleb Trippet.

Richard Tibbs.

Major Thomas P. Moore.

www.ingramcontent.com/pod-product-compliance
Lightning Source LLC
Chambersburg PA
CBHW080611270326
41928CB00016B/3000